SEX IN DRAG
BY GREG SCARNICI

FEATURING - CHRIS "GO GO" HARDER, DALLAS DUBOIS, LOGAN HARDCORE and JOHNNY POOL

AND INTRODUCING - DANE ANTHONY, CHRIS CALDWELL, QUAMIN ELLIS, GLENN PAYNE, JAY ROTH, DUSTIN WHITLEY and CONRAD WOOLFE

PHOTOGRAPHY - WILSON MODELS
WIG STYLIST - SANDRA LAWRENCE
MAKEUP - STEPHEN WORKMAN
GRAPHIC ARTISTS - DEPUTY DIRTYLEGS and CHRIS PURCELL

EDITED BY DEPUTY DIRTYLEGS

SHOT ENTIRELY IN CHERRY GROVE, FIRE ISLAND.

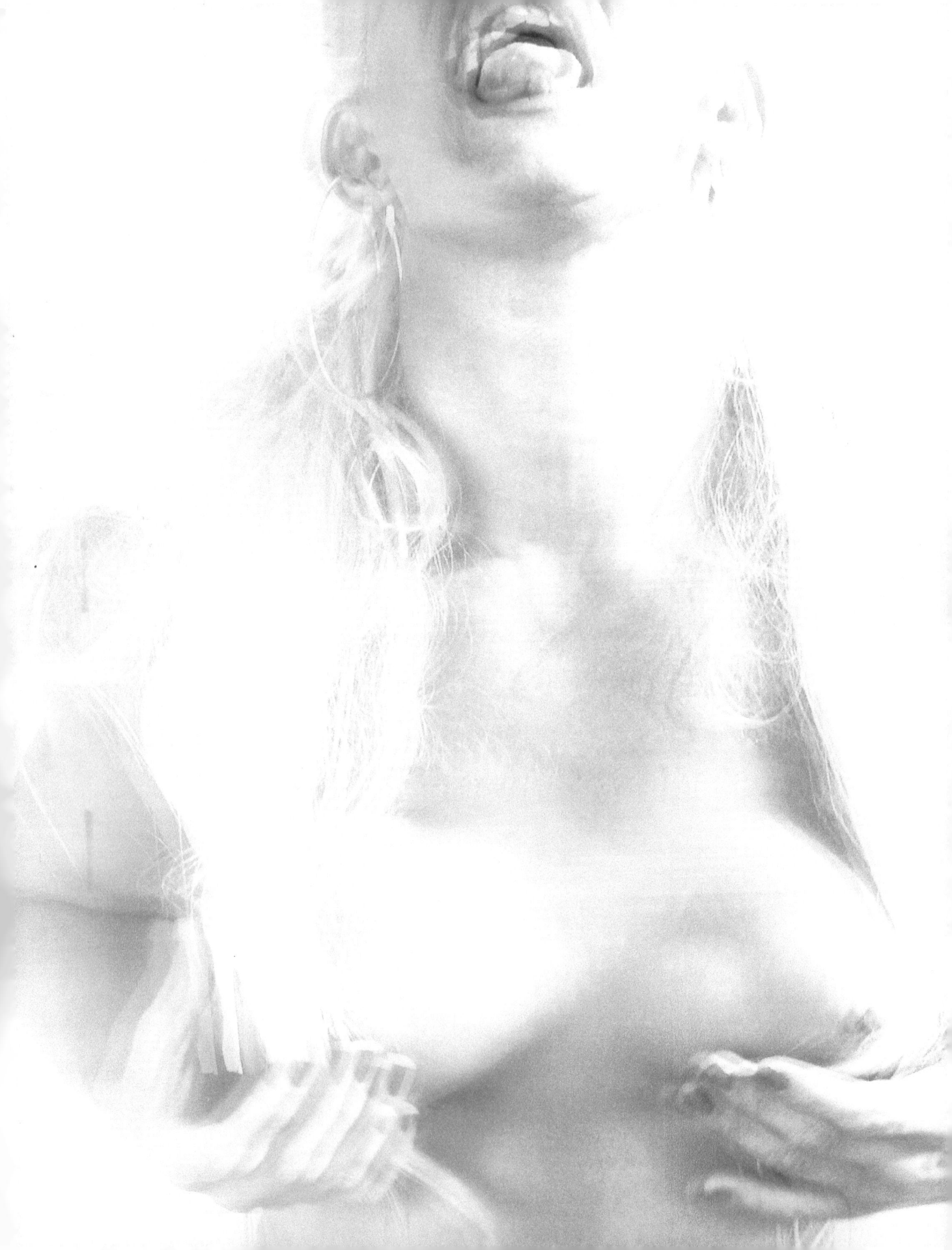

My name is Chita.
I'll be your drag queen tonight.
I like to wear girls underpants...
Even when I shave my stubble
I kinda look like Barney Rubble
But once you have that shot of Jaeger
I'll stop looking like Schwarzenegger
But something tells me you don't care
That my real name is Pierre
Because you're right down on your knees.
About to catch a venereal disease.

Come with me.
Back to my place.
Do it now.
Before I use mace.
Come with me.
Don't be a schmuck.
So come with me...

I'll teach you how to tuck.

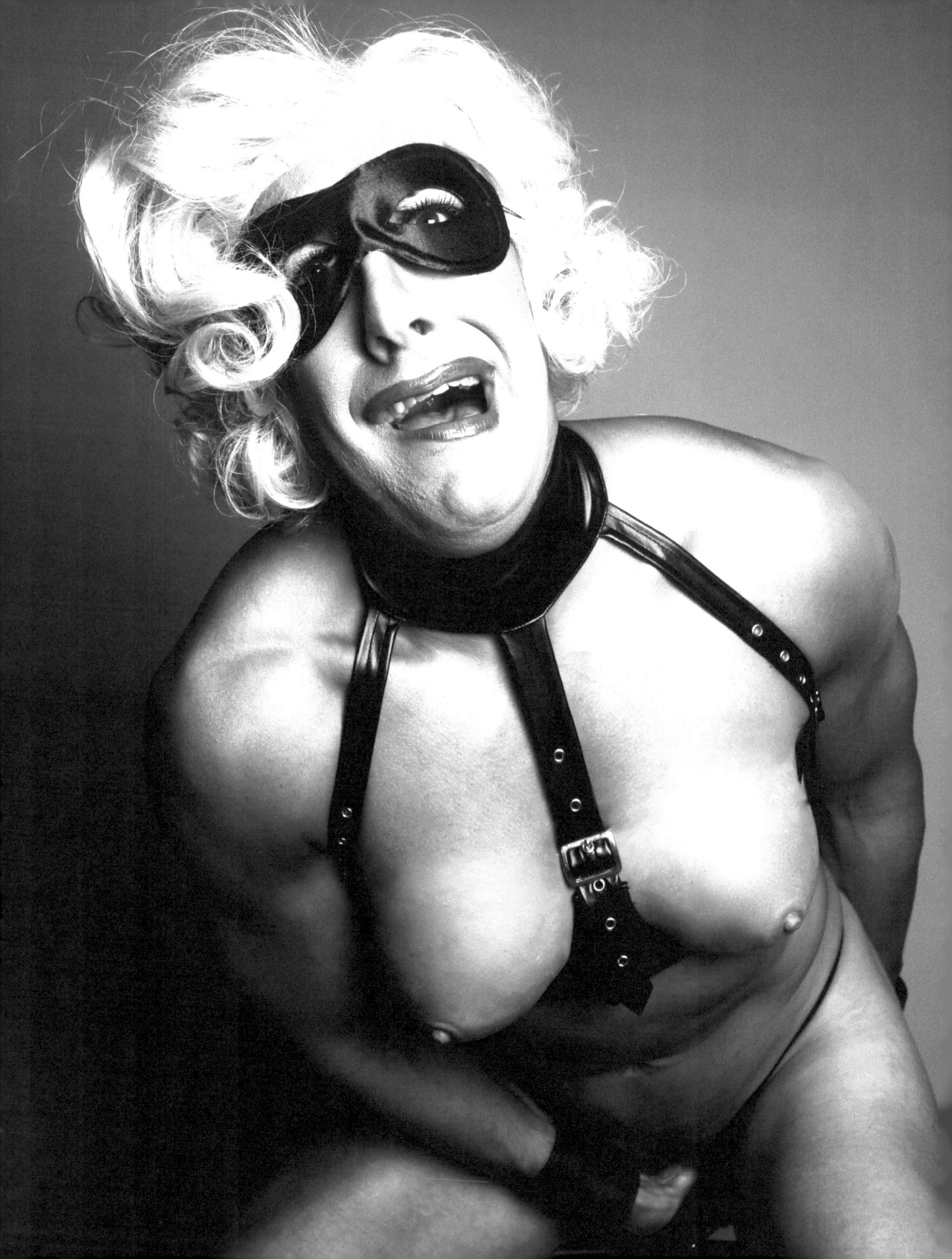

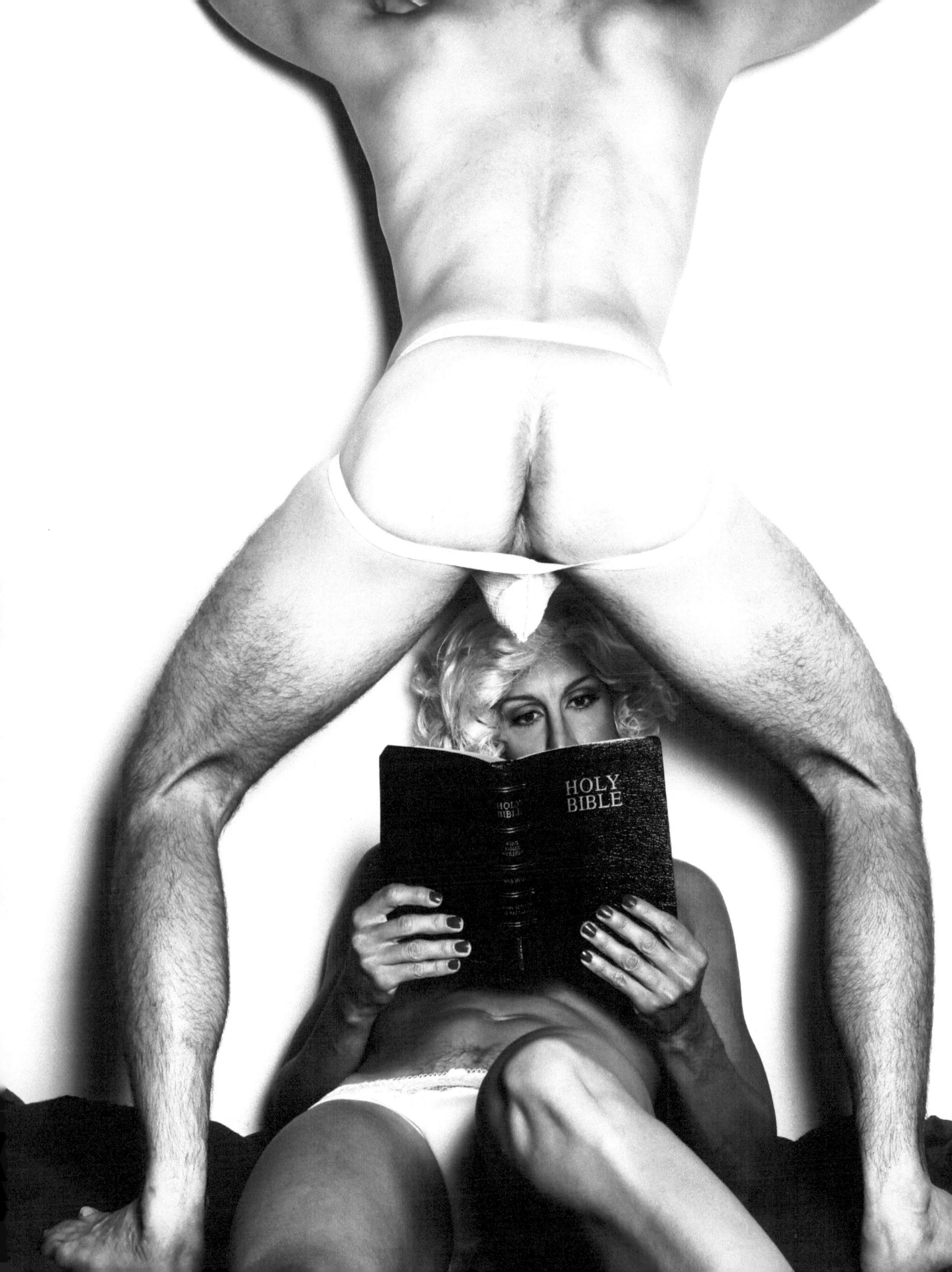

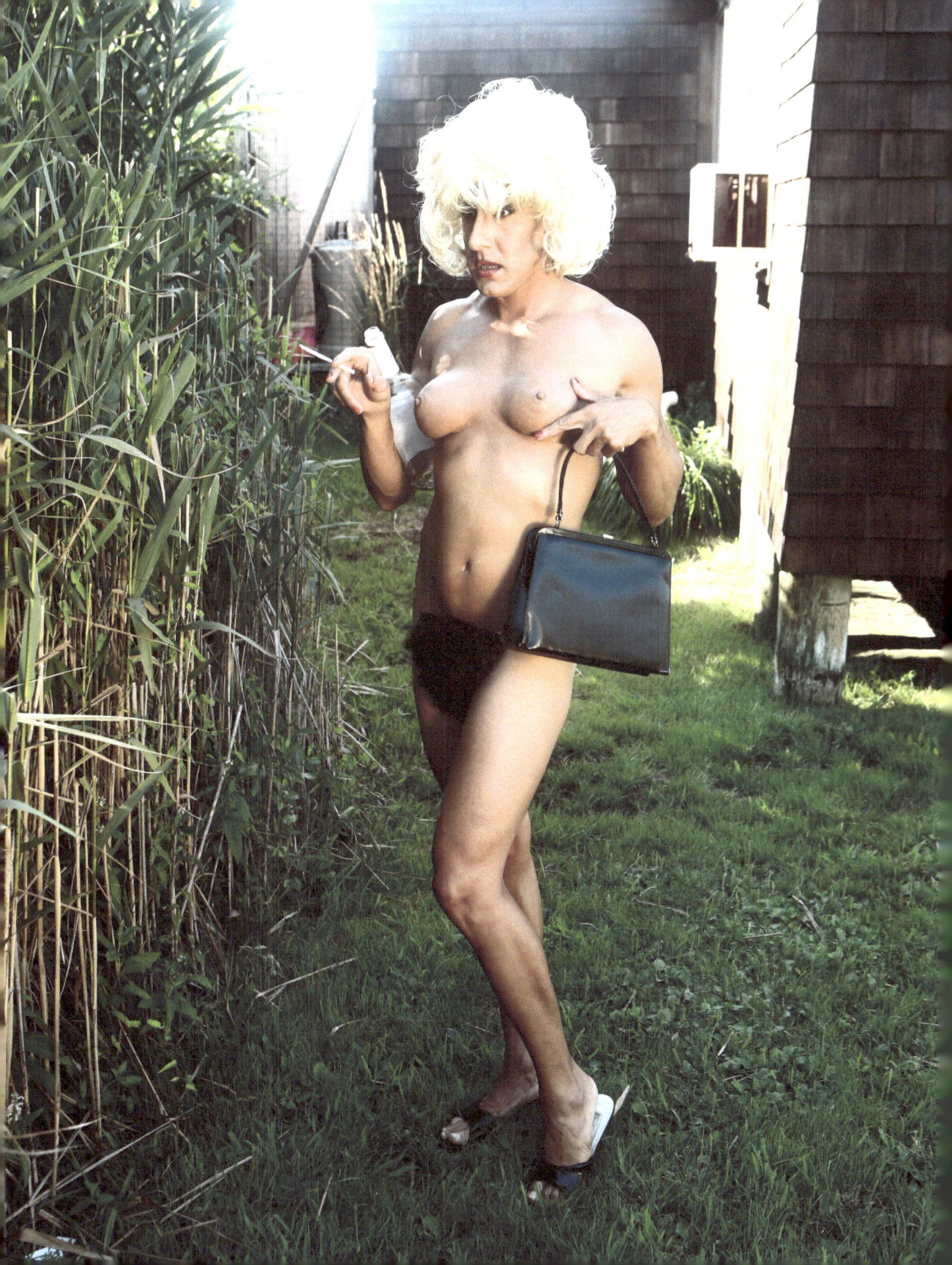

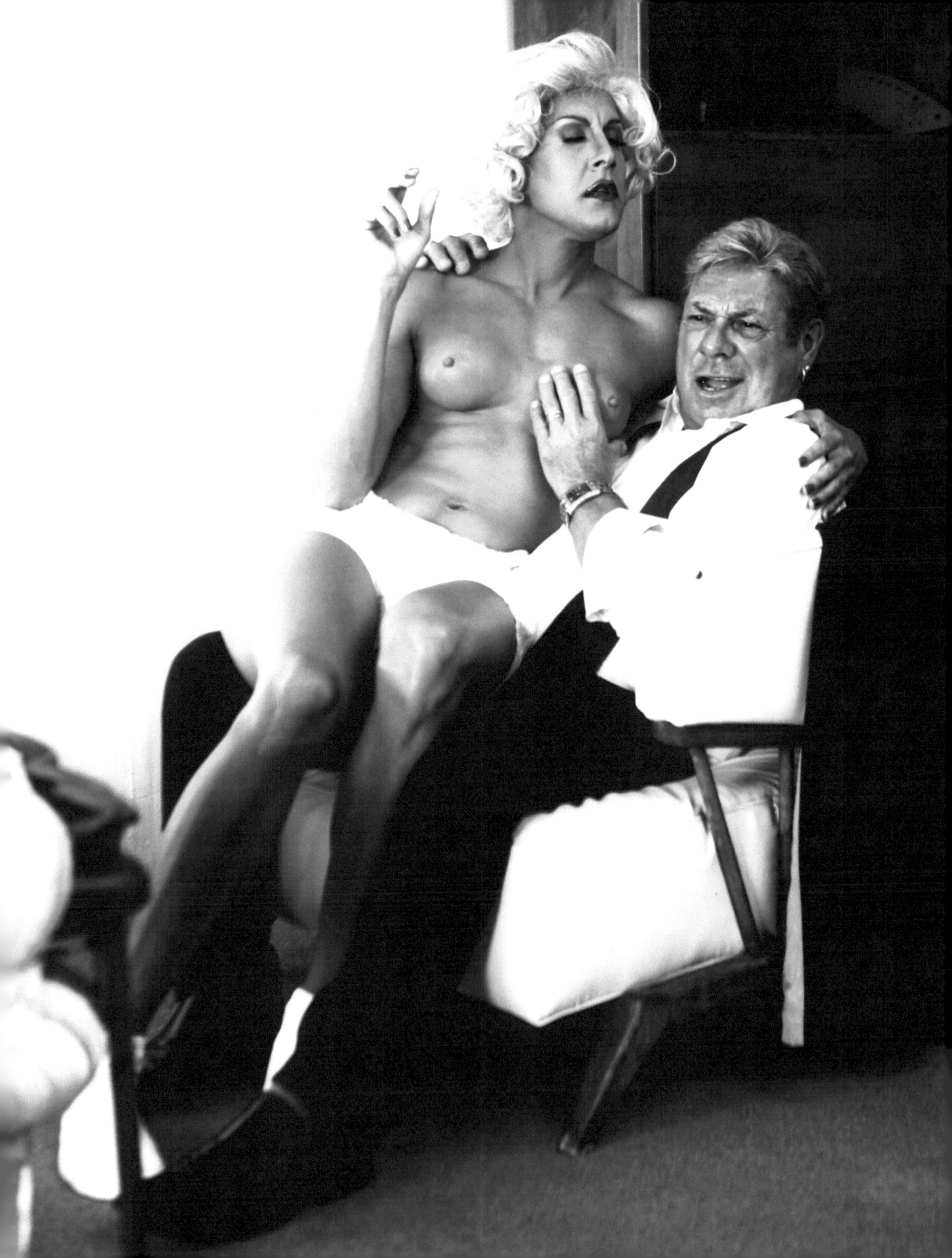

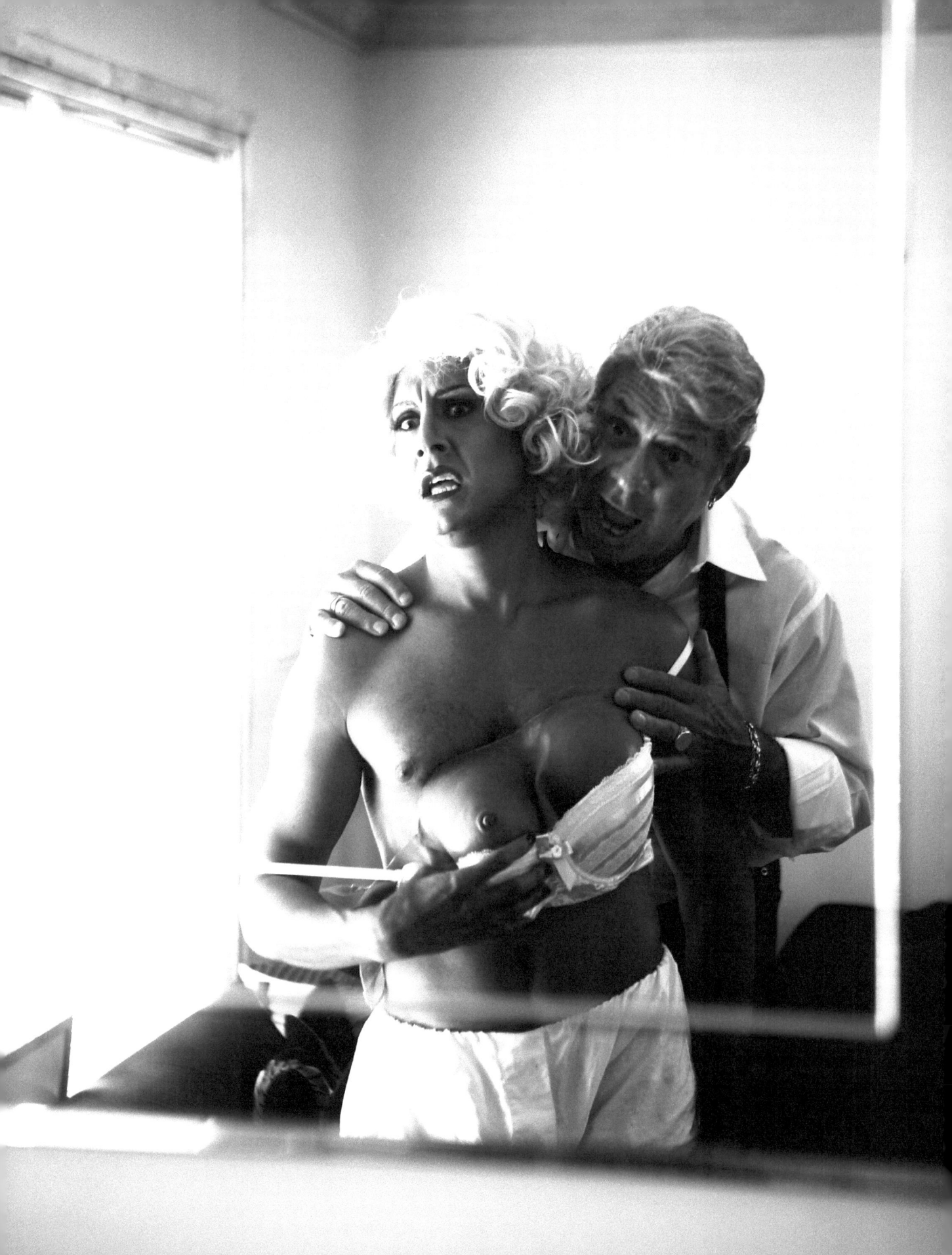

Oooooh! Aaaaah!

Eeeeee!

Oooooo!

My boobies are so sensitive!

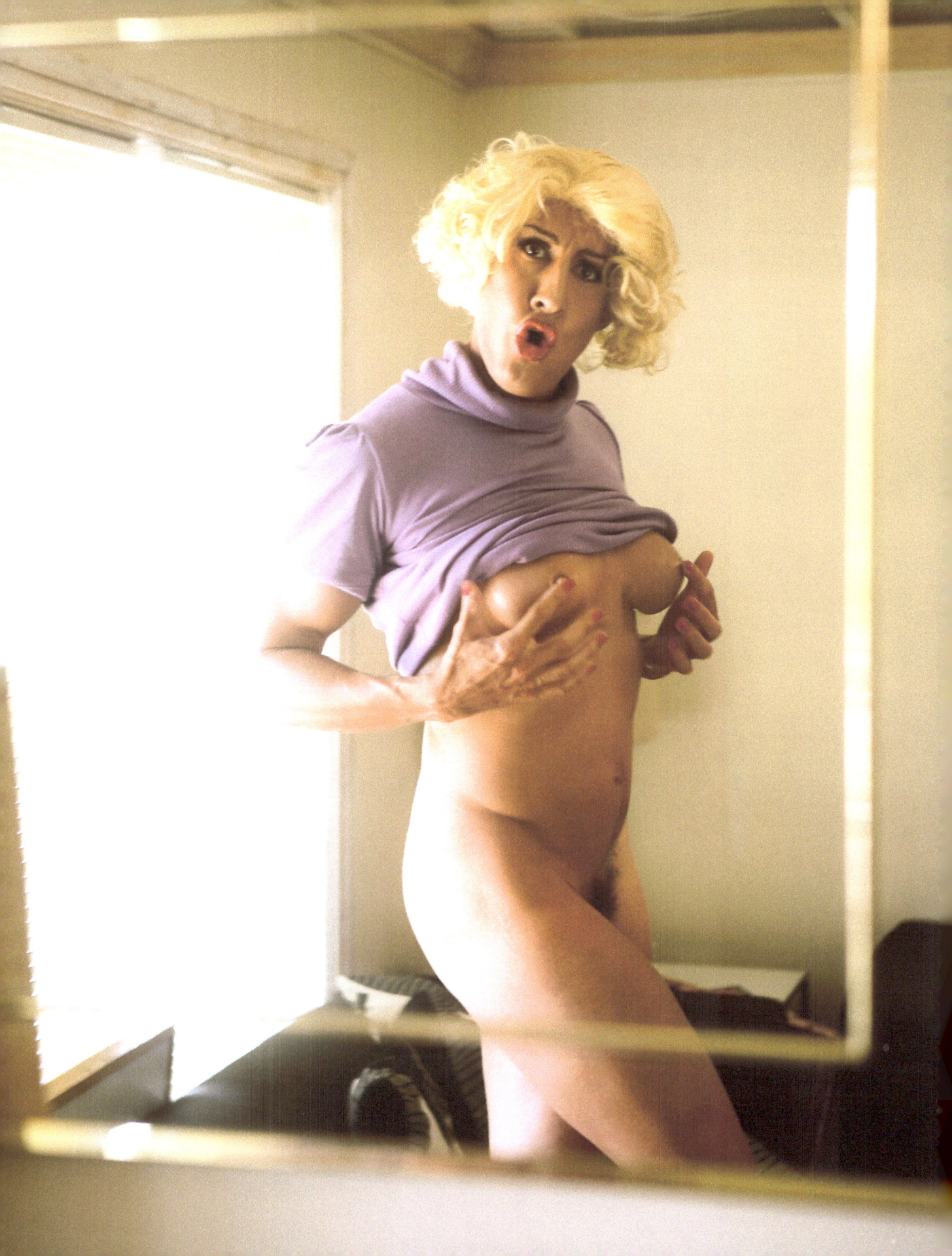

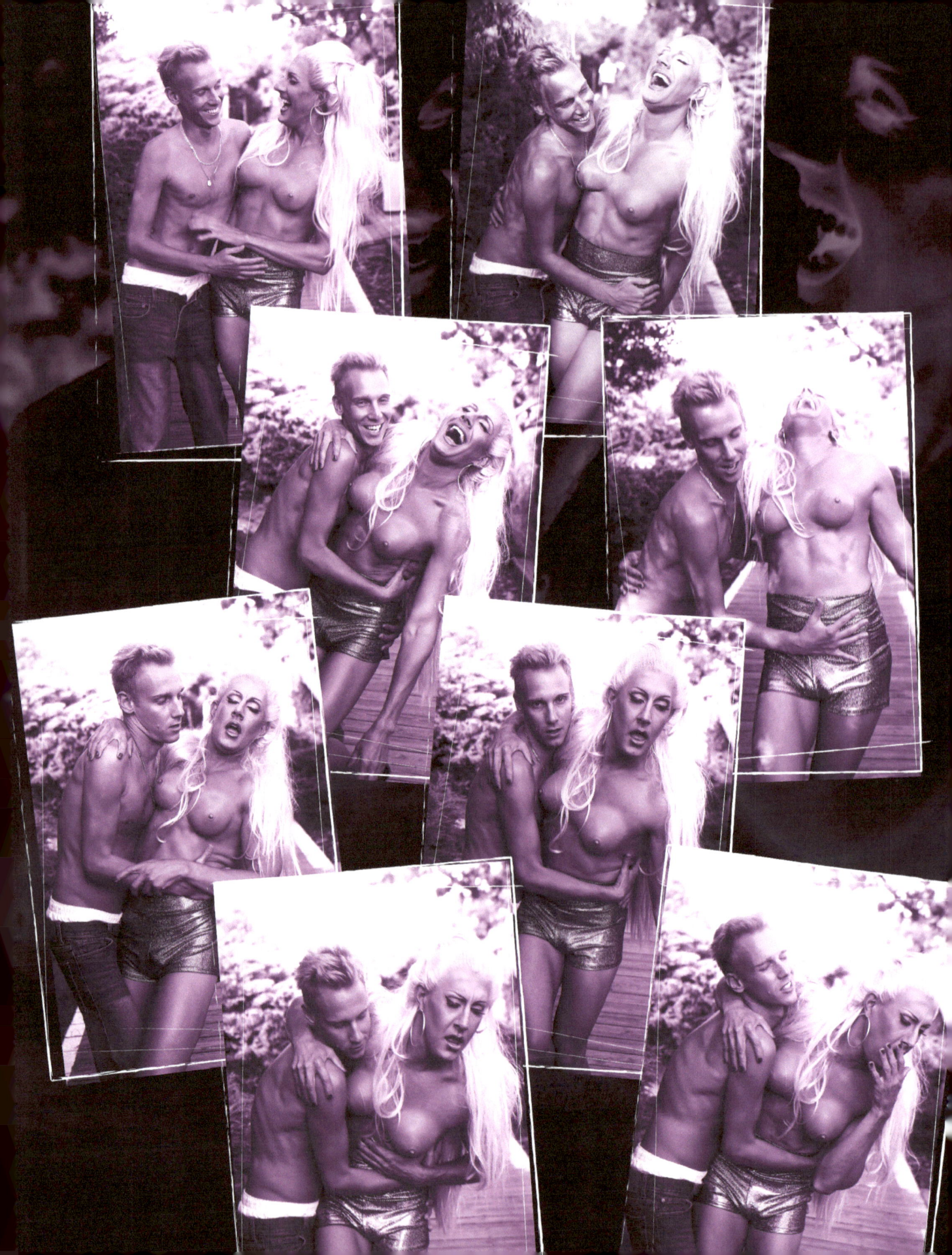

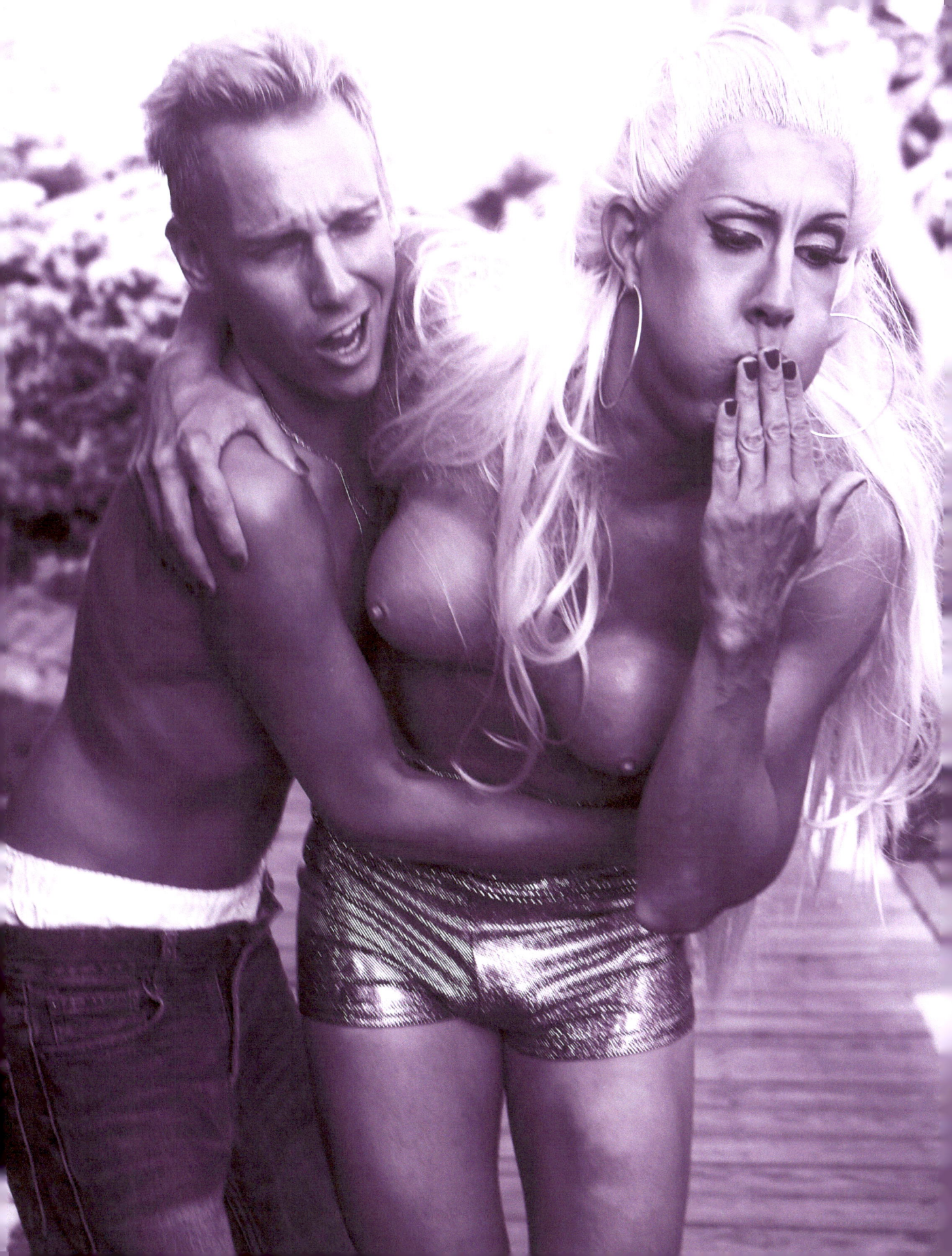

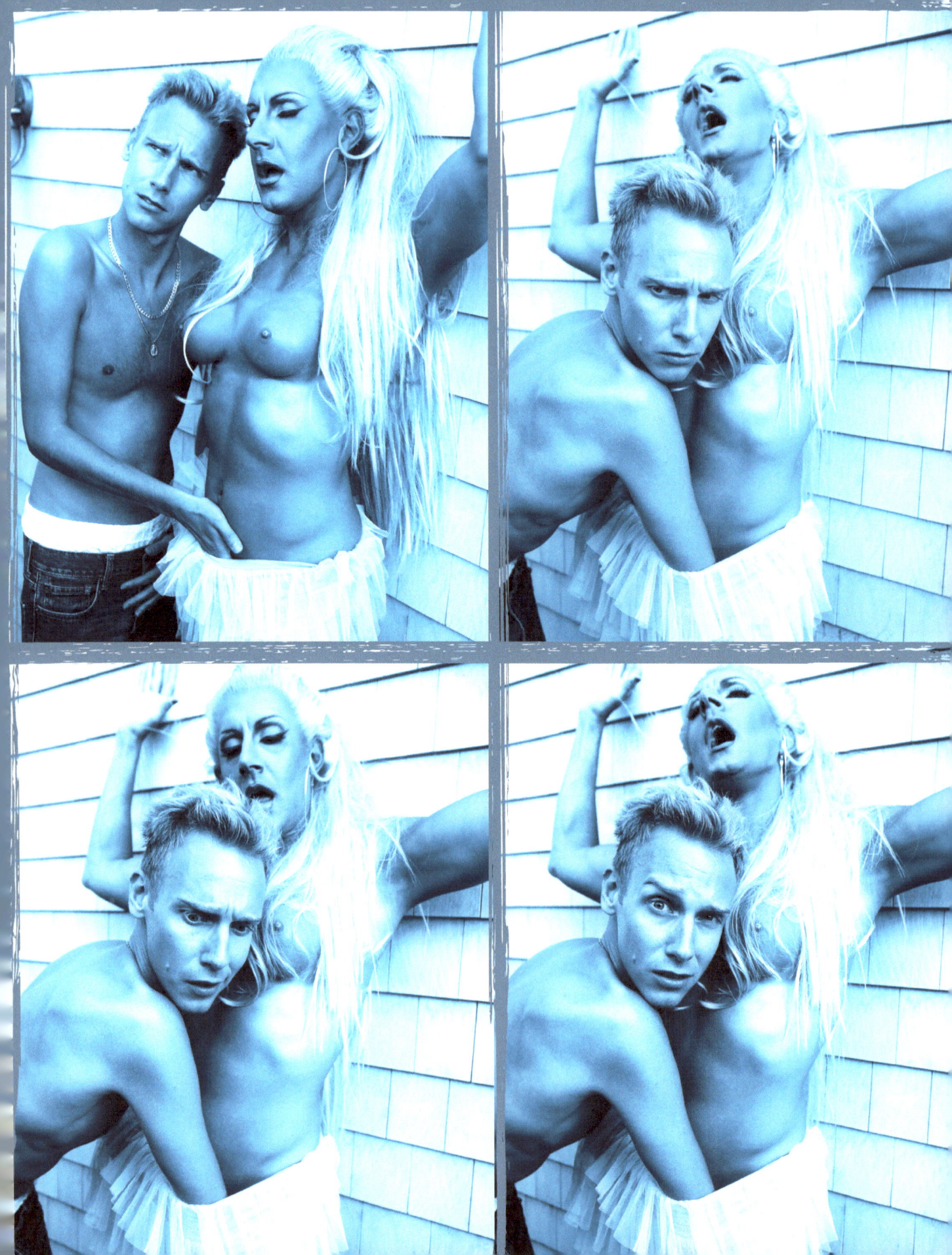

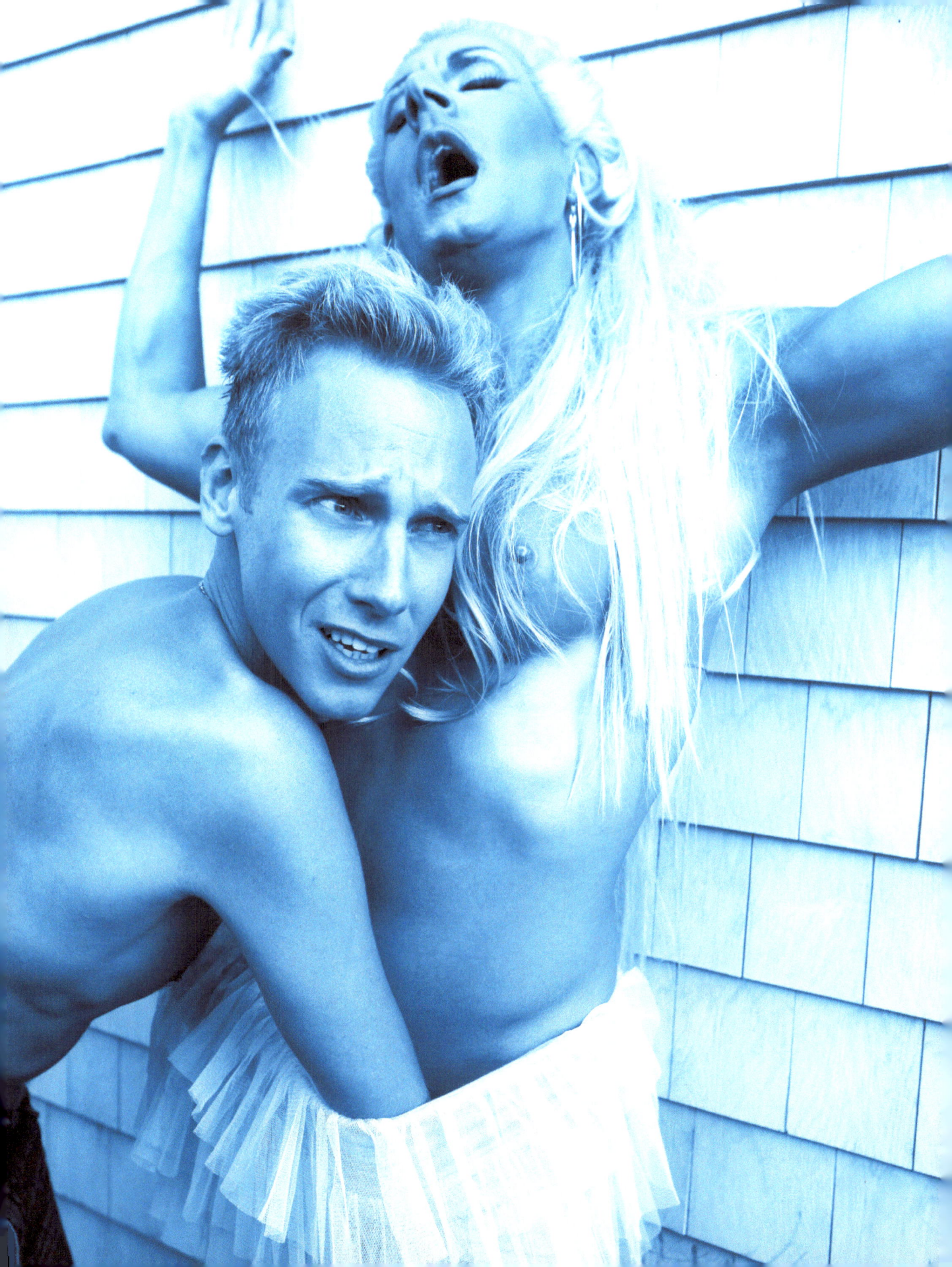

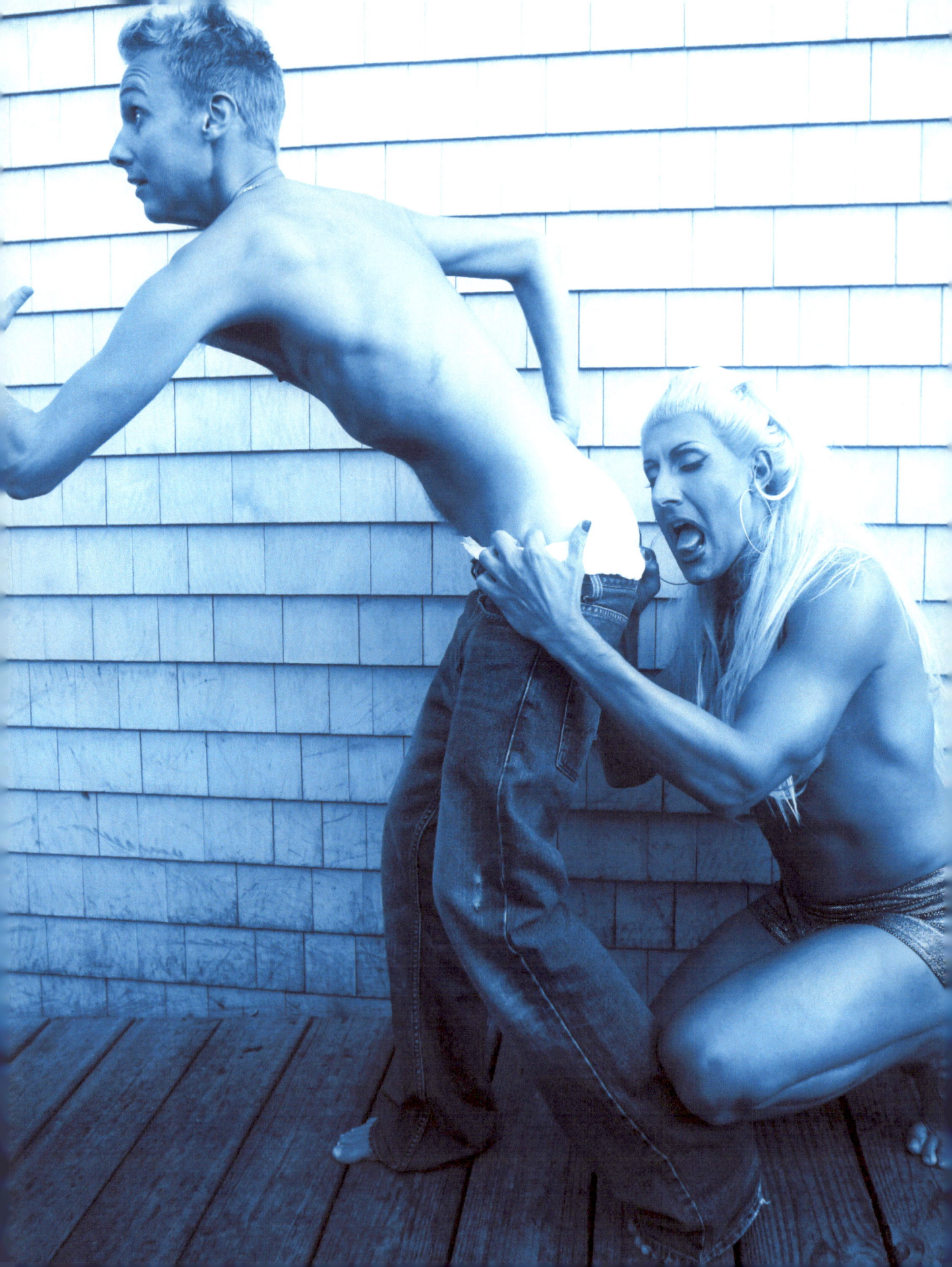

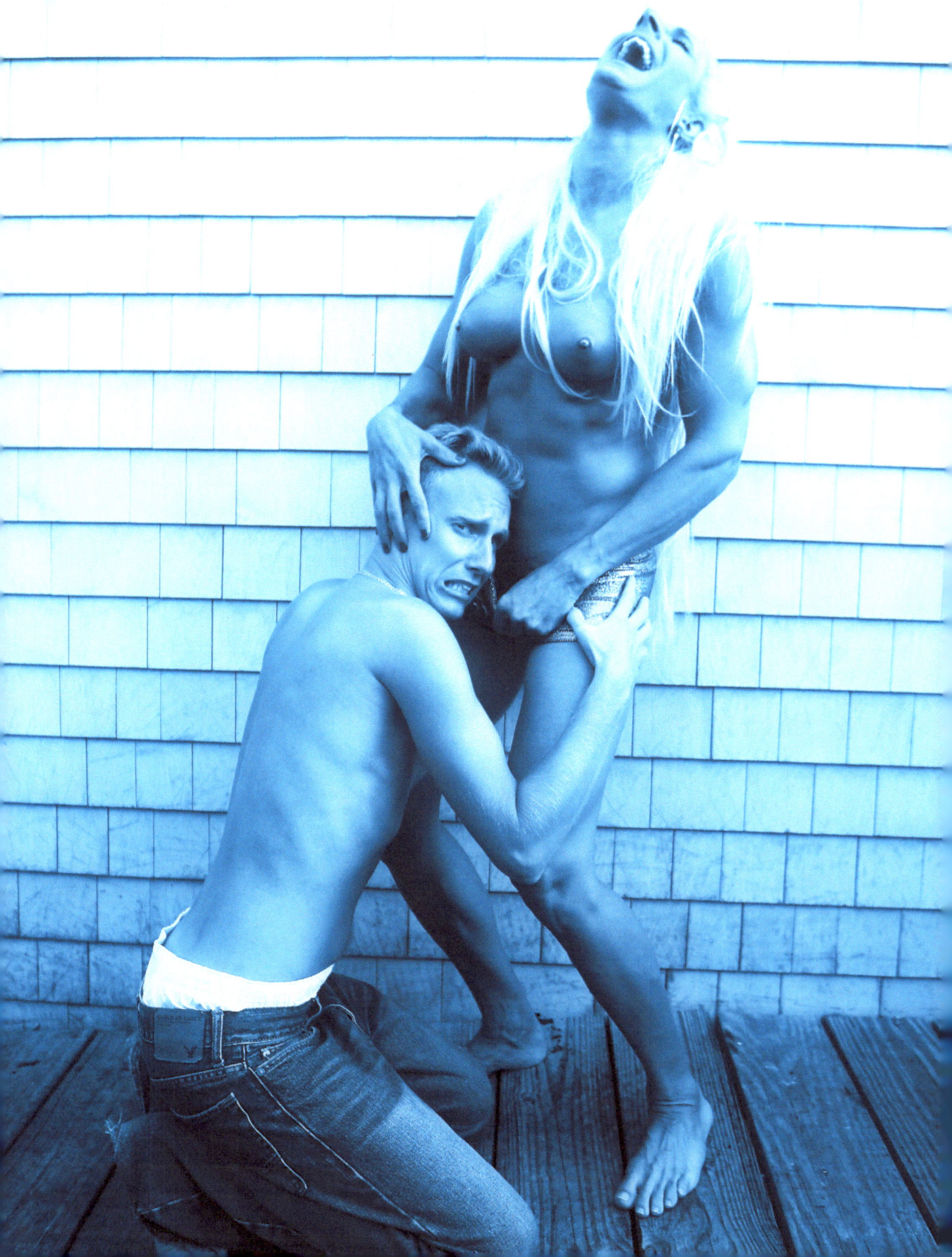

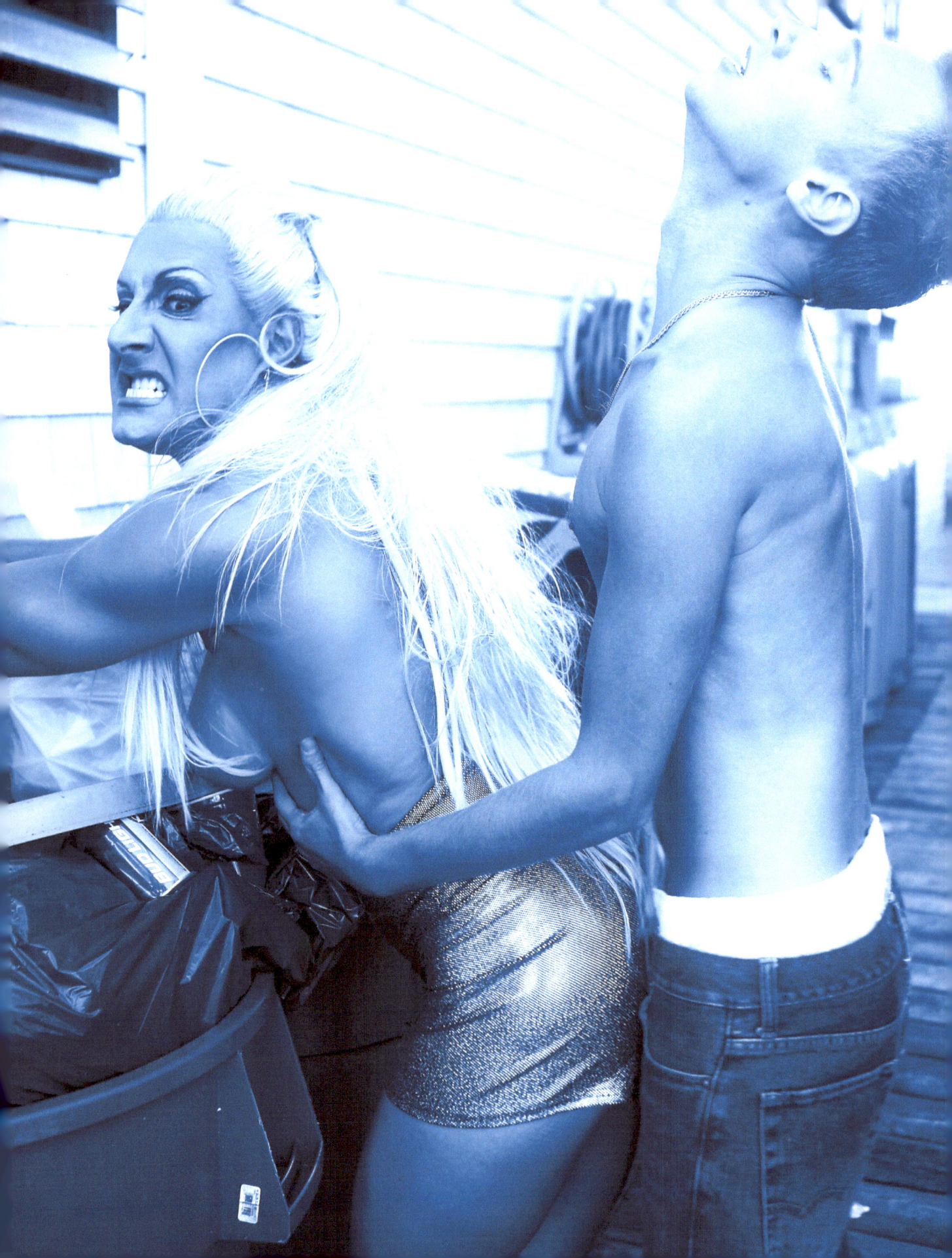

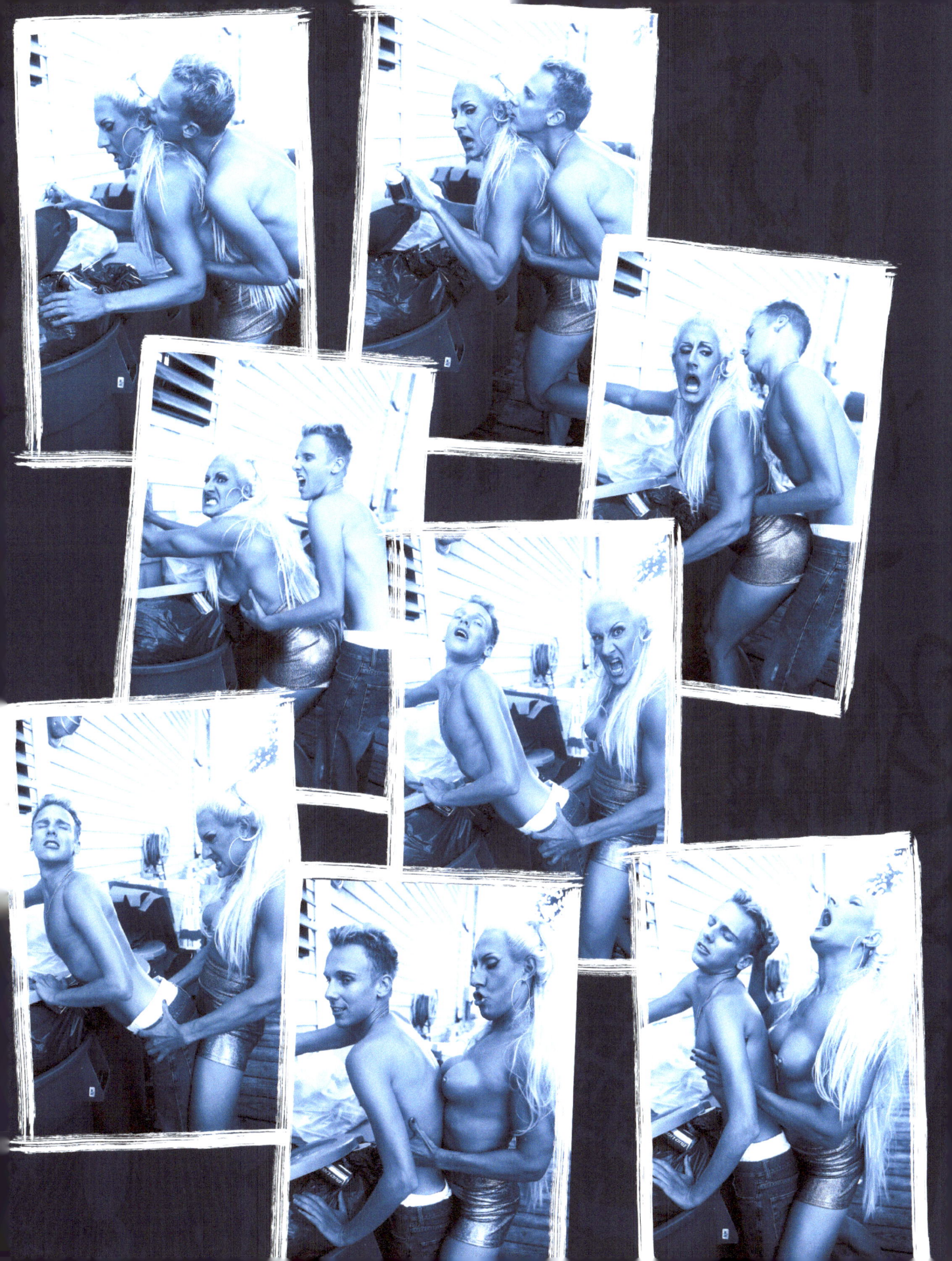

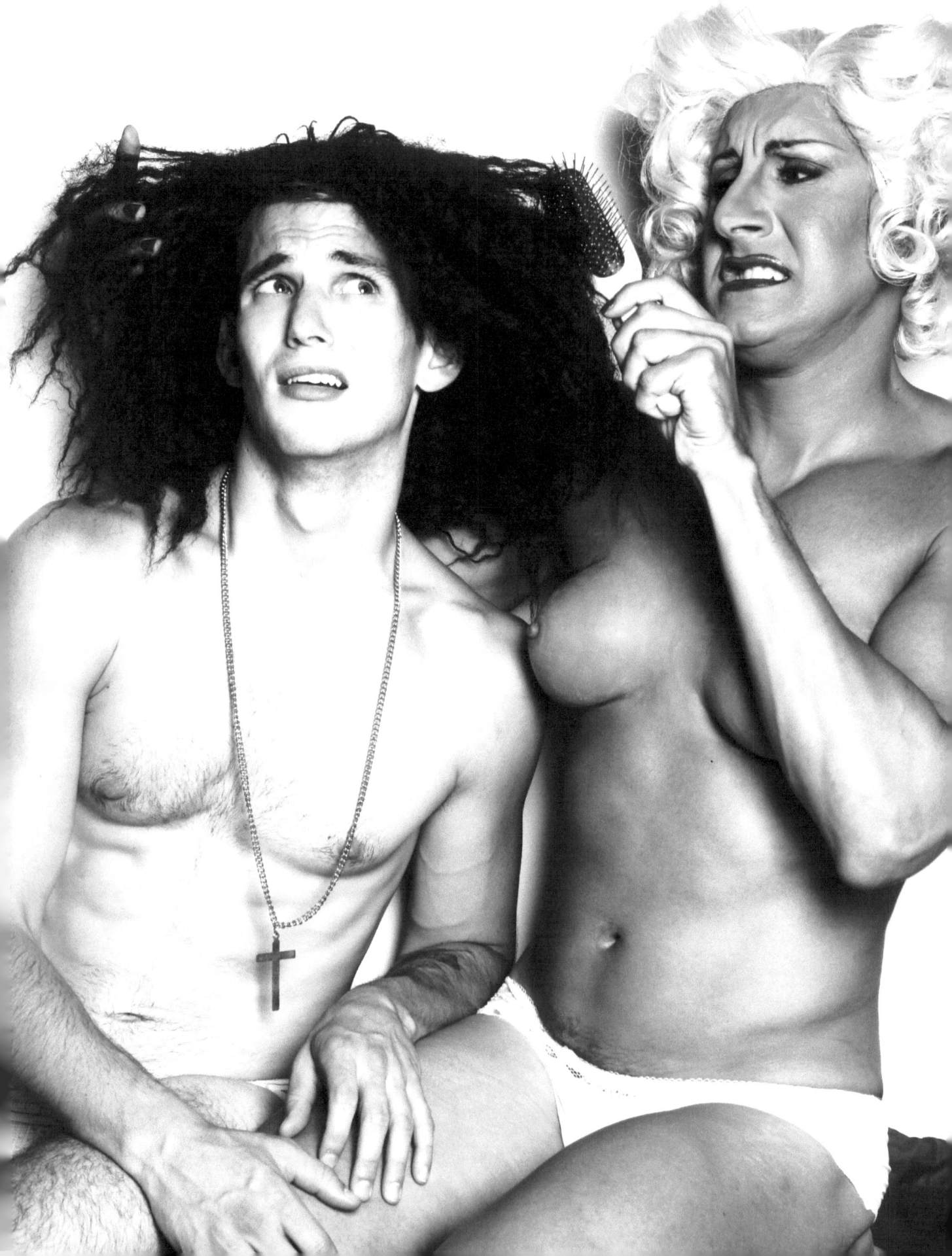

Dear Johnny,

There's no way in hell I'm shooting our sex tape with your hair all dry and nasty-looking. I mean, what did you think, showing up with your hair all fried up, looking like some kind of homeless?

And don't pretend you haven't heard this before. I distinctly remember the last time you came over to munch my mussy, when I said you needed to pick up some Donny's Hair Rejuvenator, or give yourself a hot oil treatment. Right now, I am so turned off, my hole is drier than your hair! So if you want my mangina moist again, you'd better start using conditioner.

Yours truly,
Chita

PS: I will comb you out this time, but that's just because we're meeting my mother for dinner at the Olive Garden.

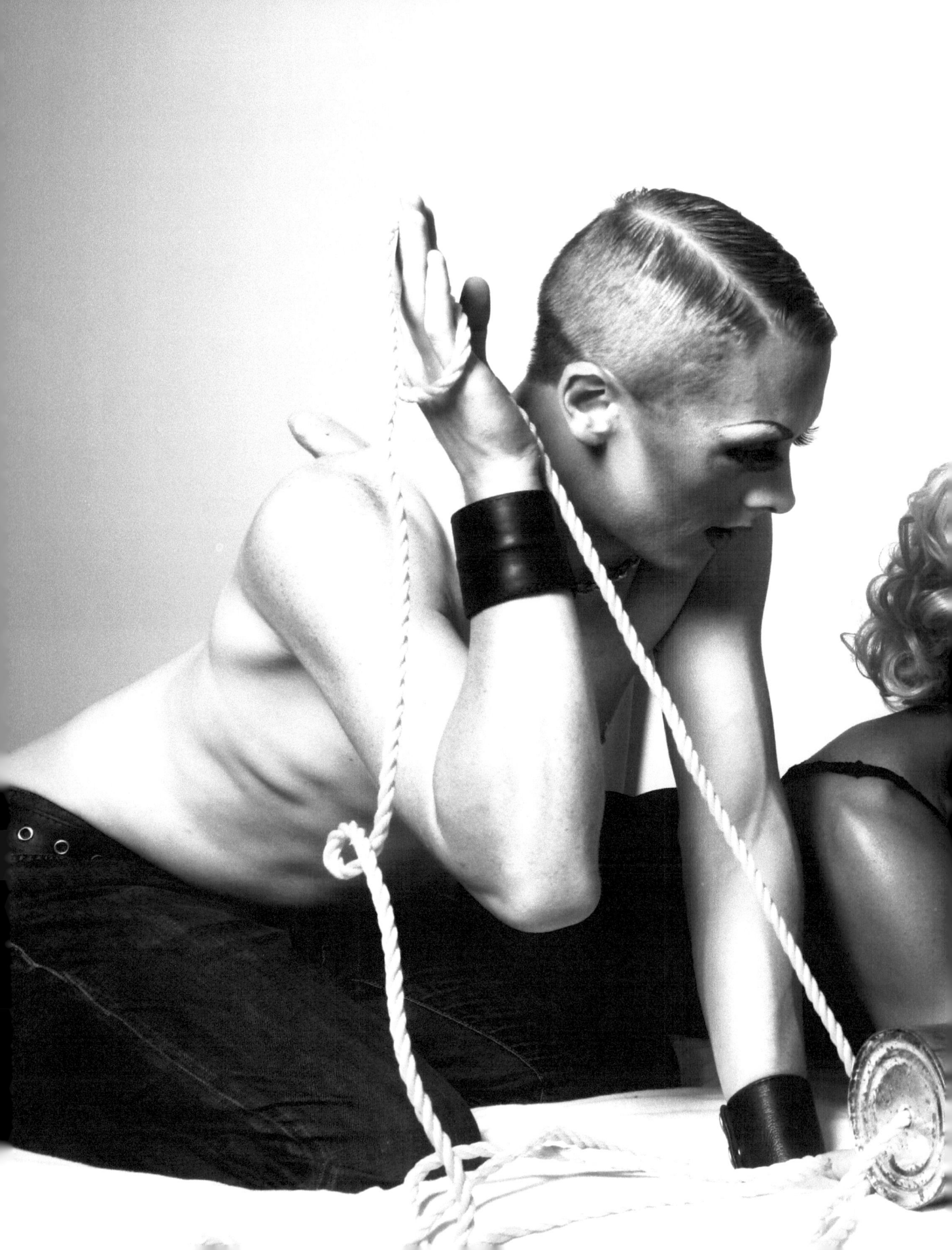

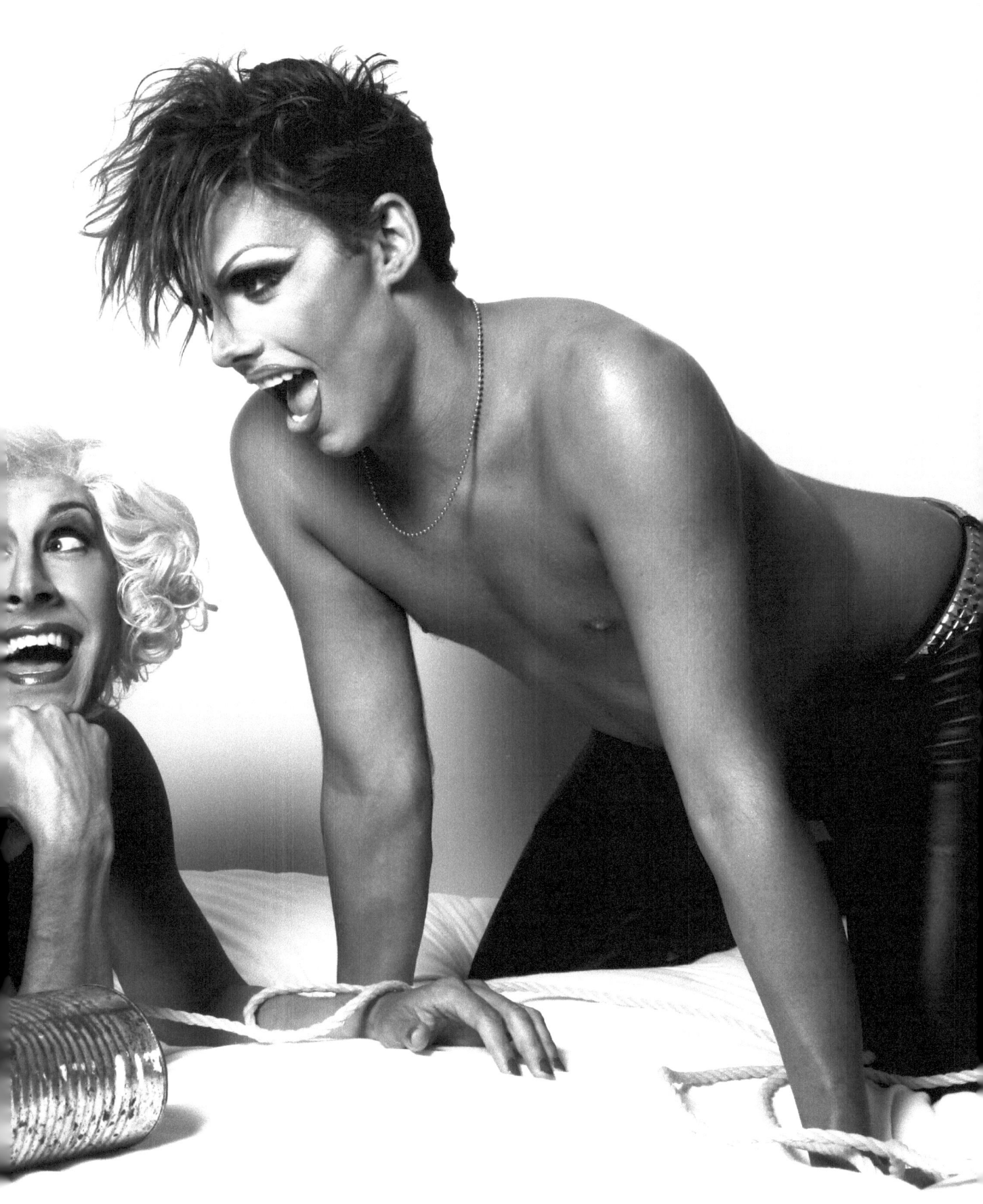

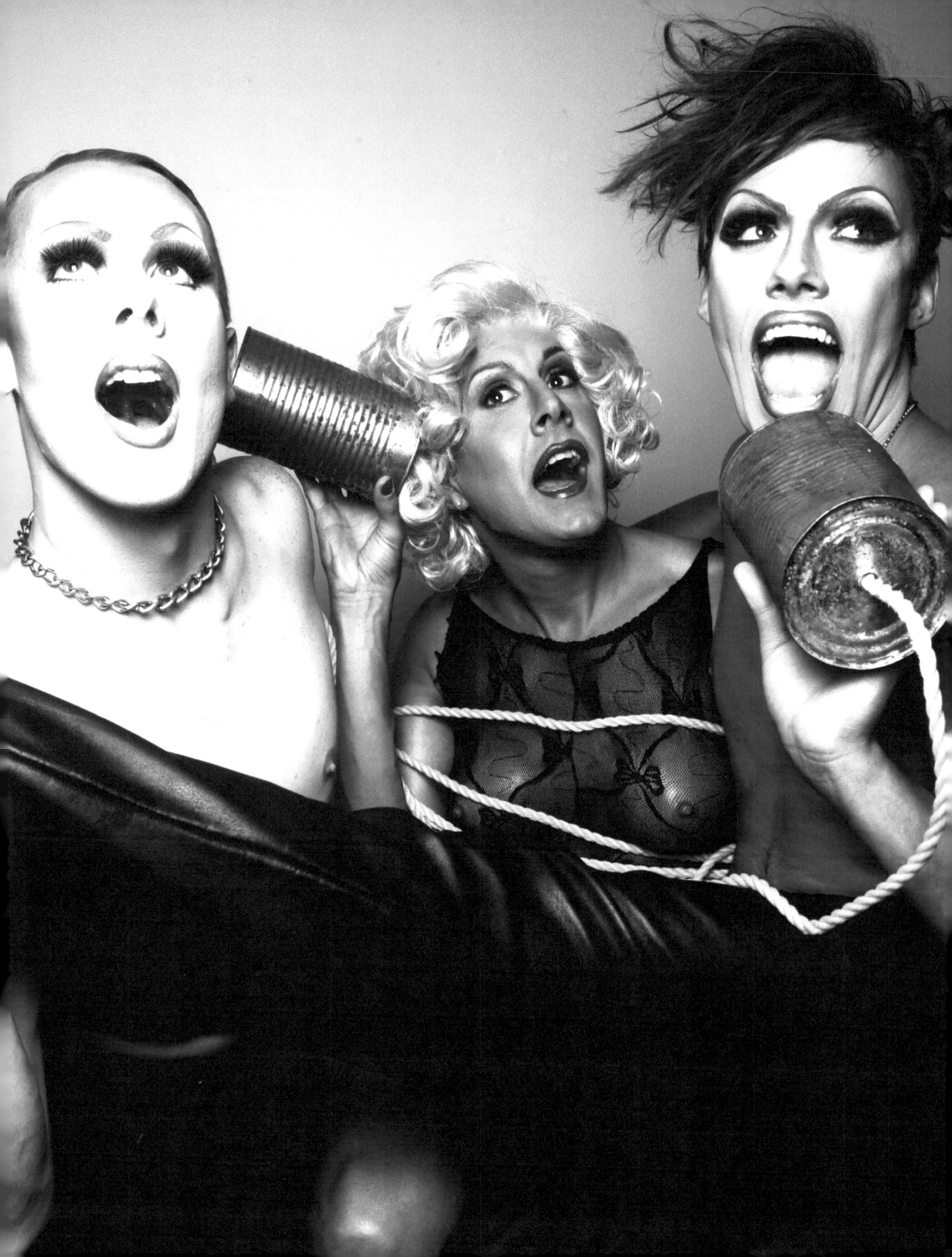

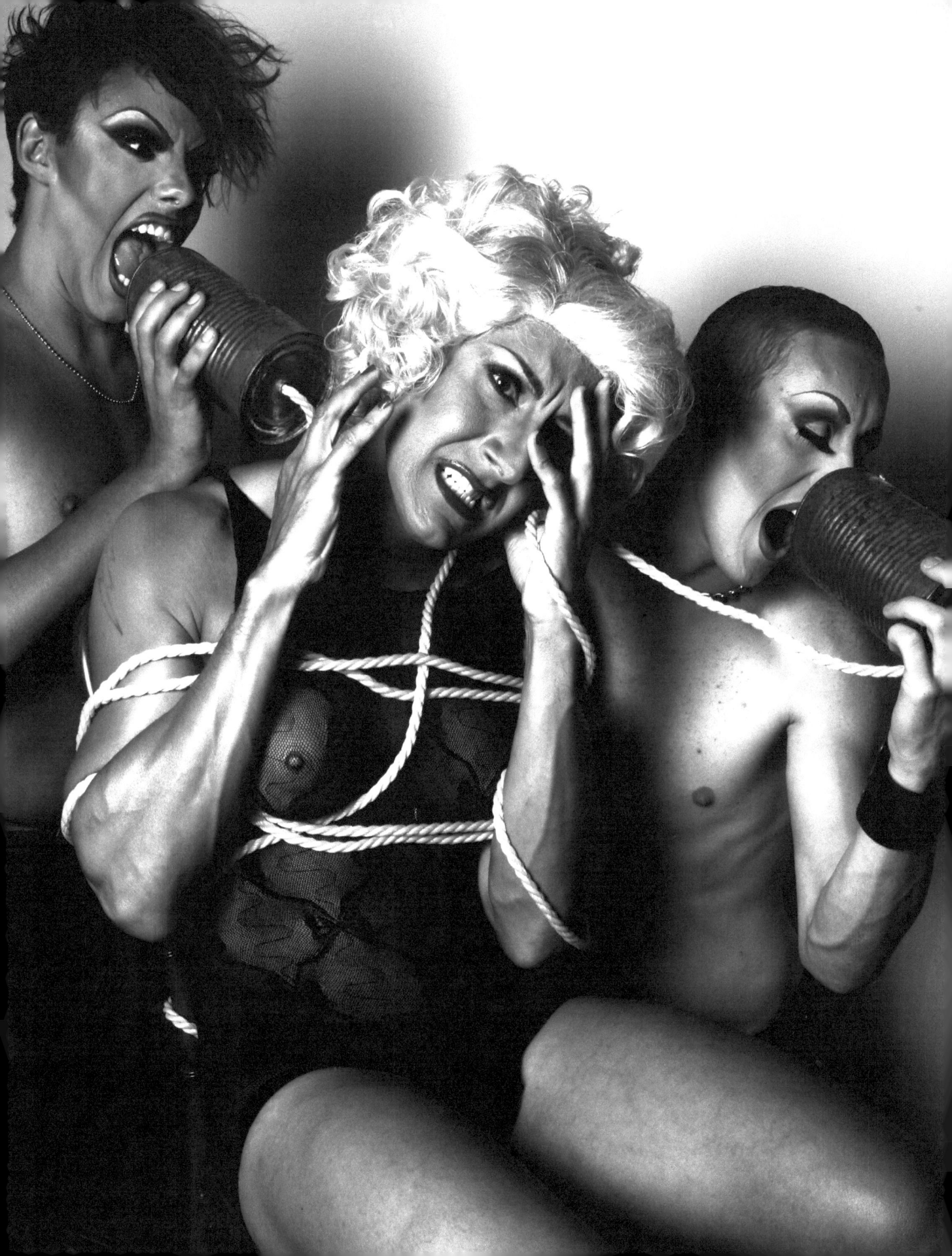

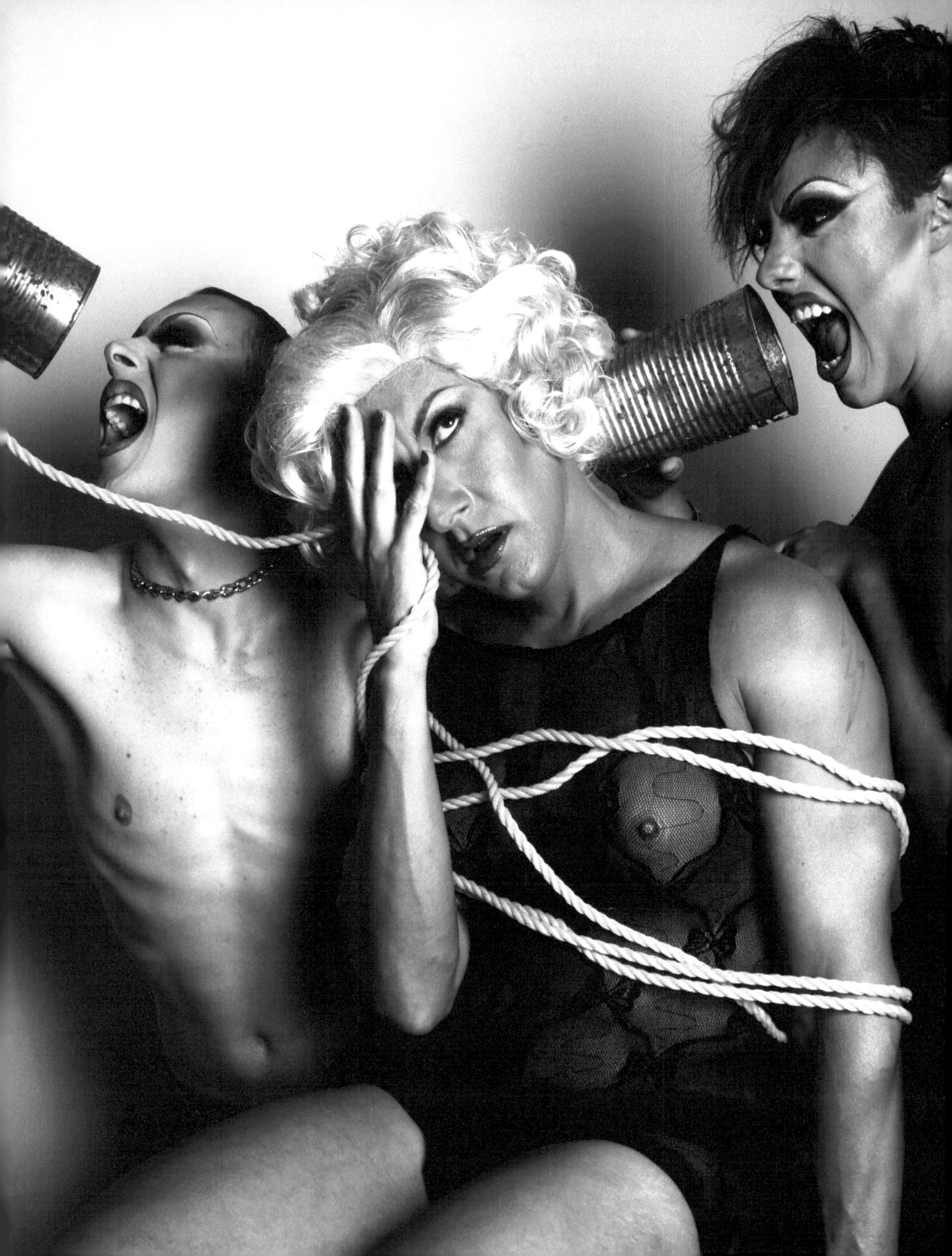

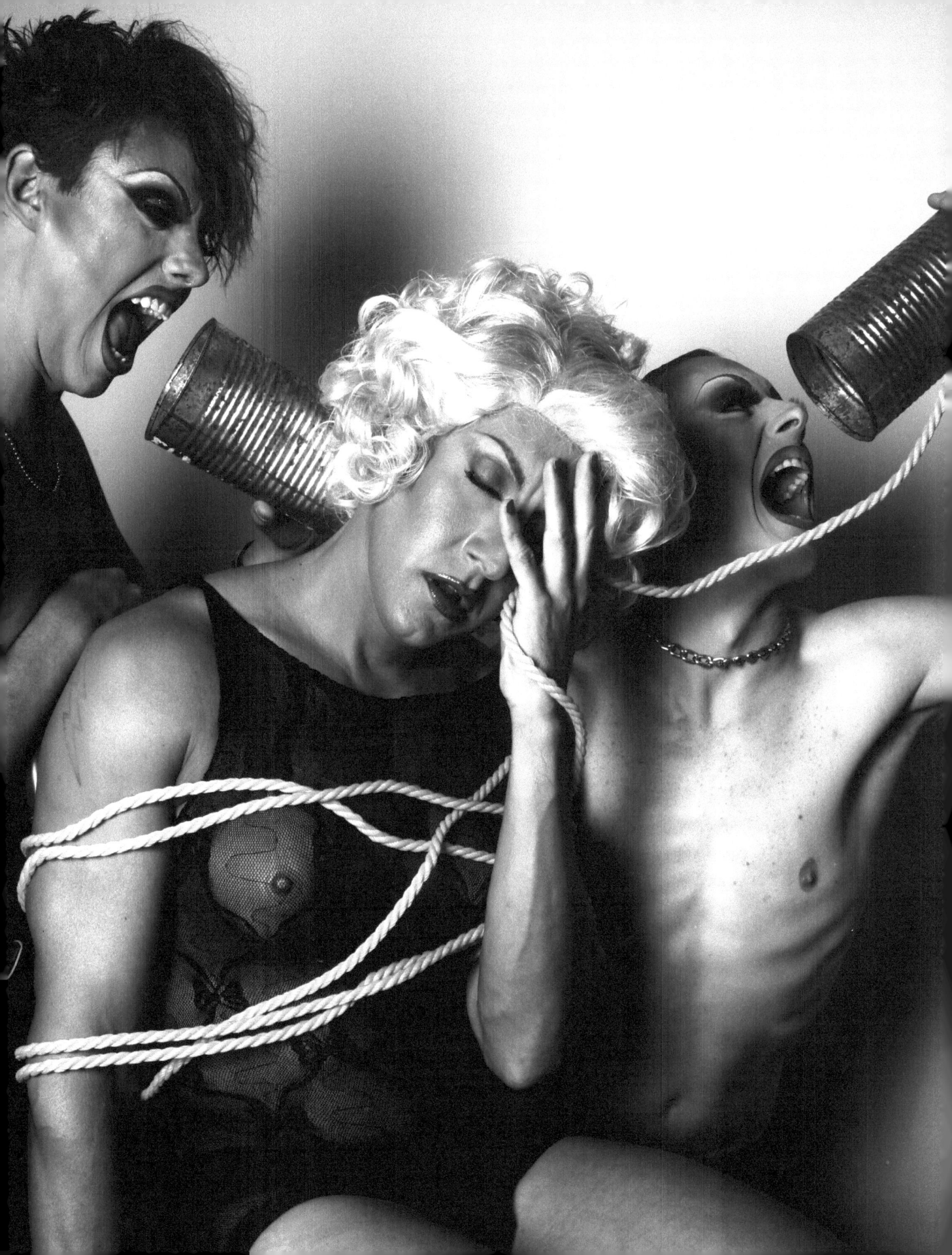

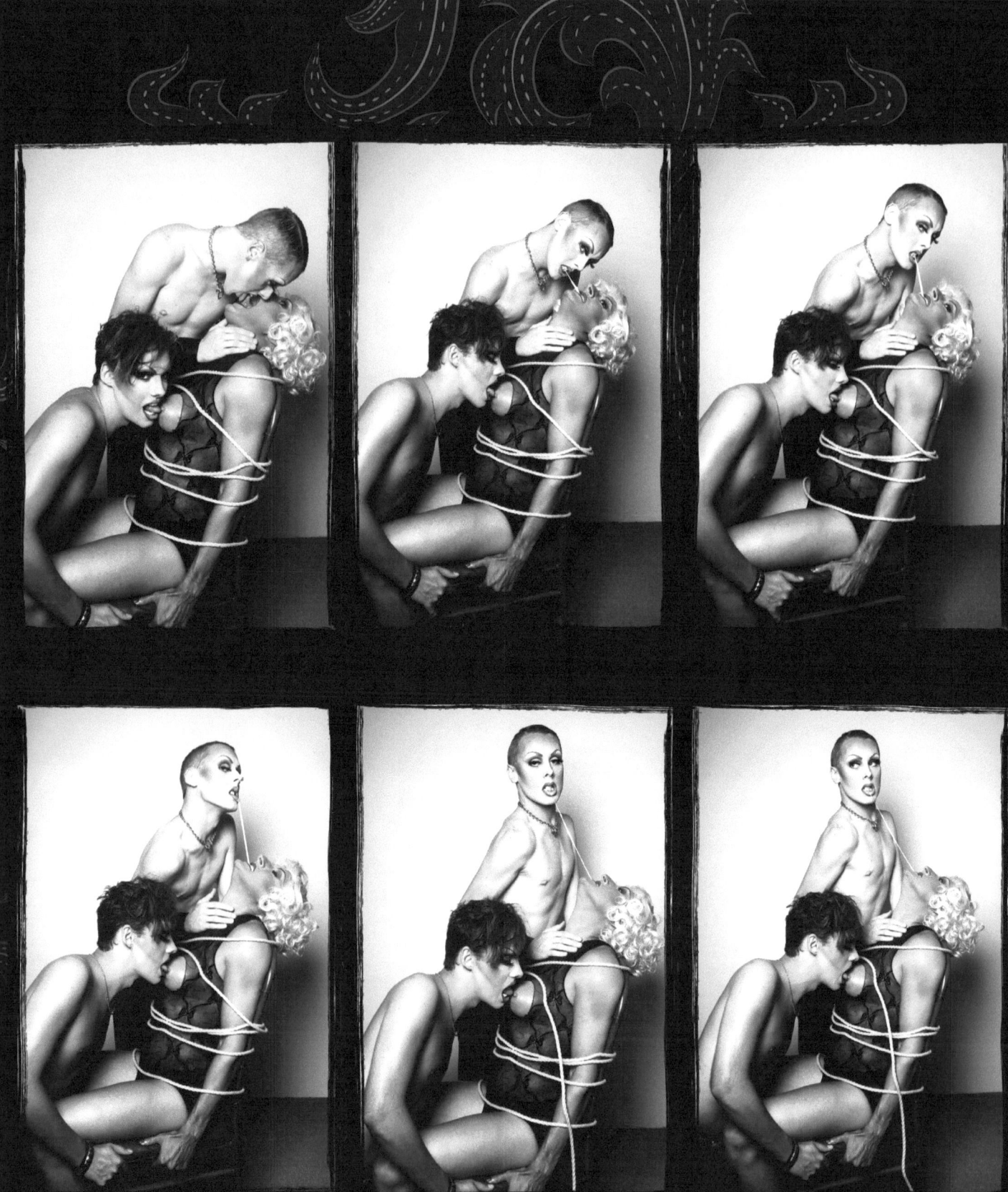

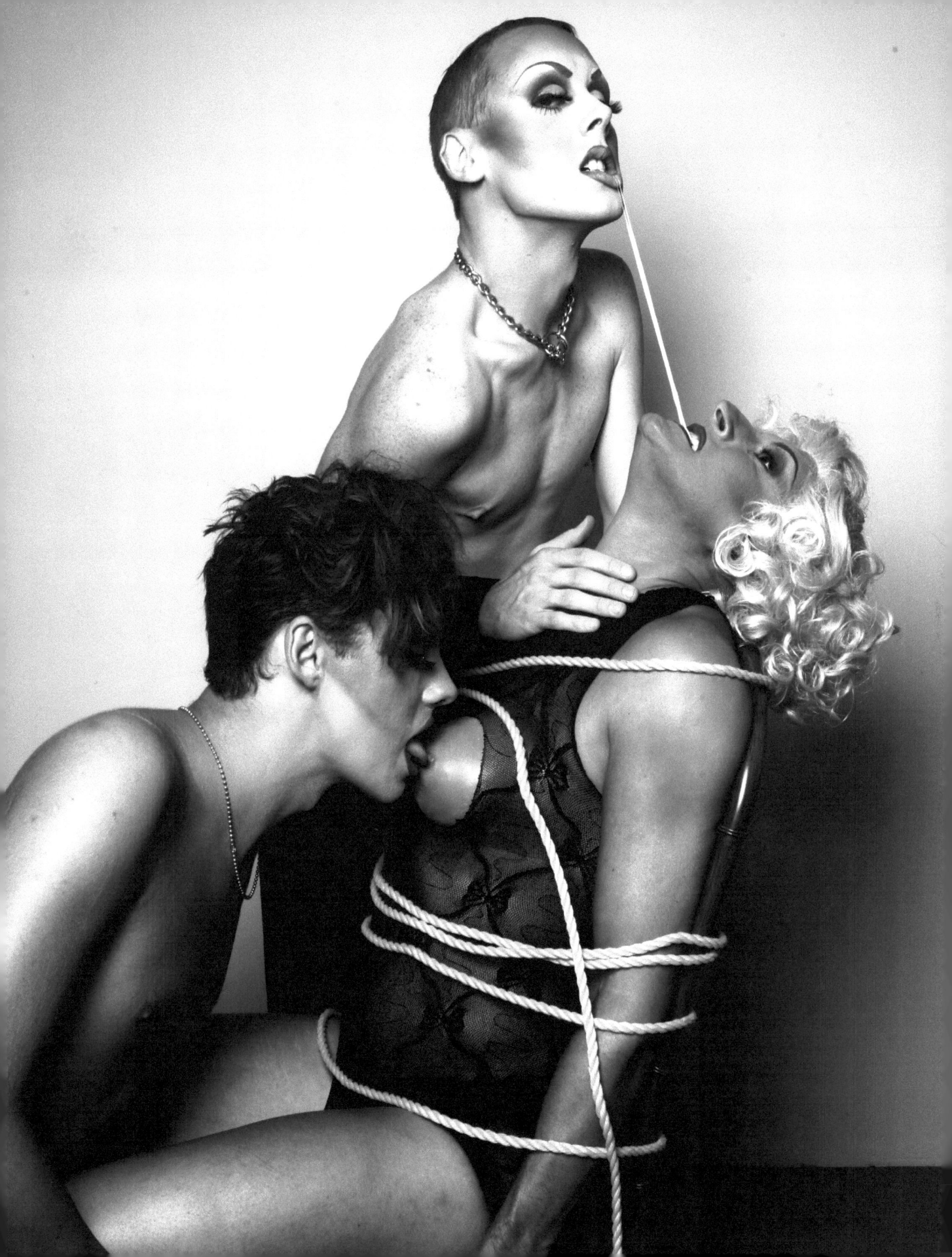

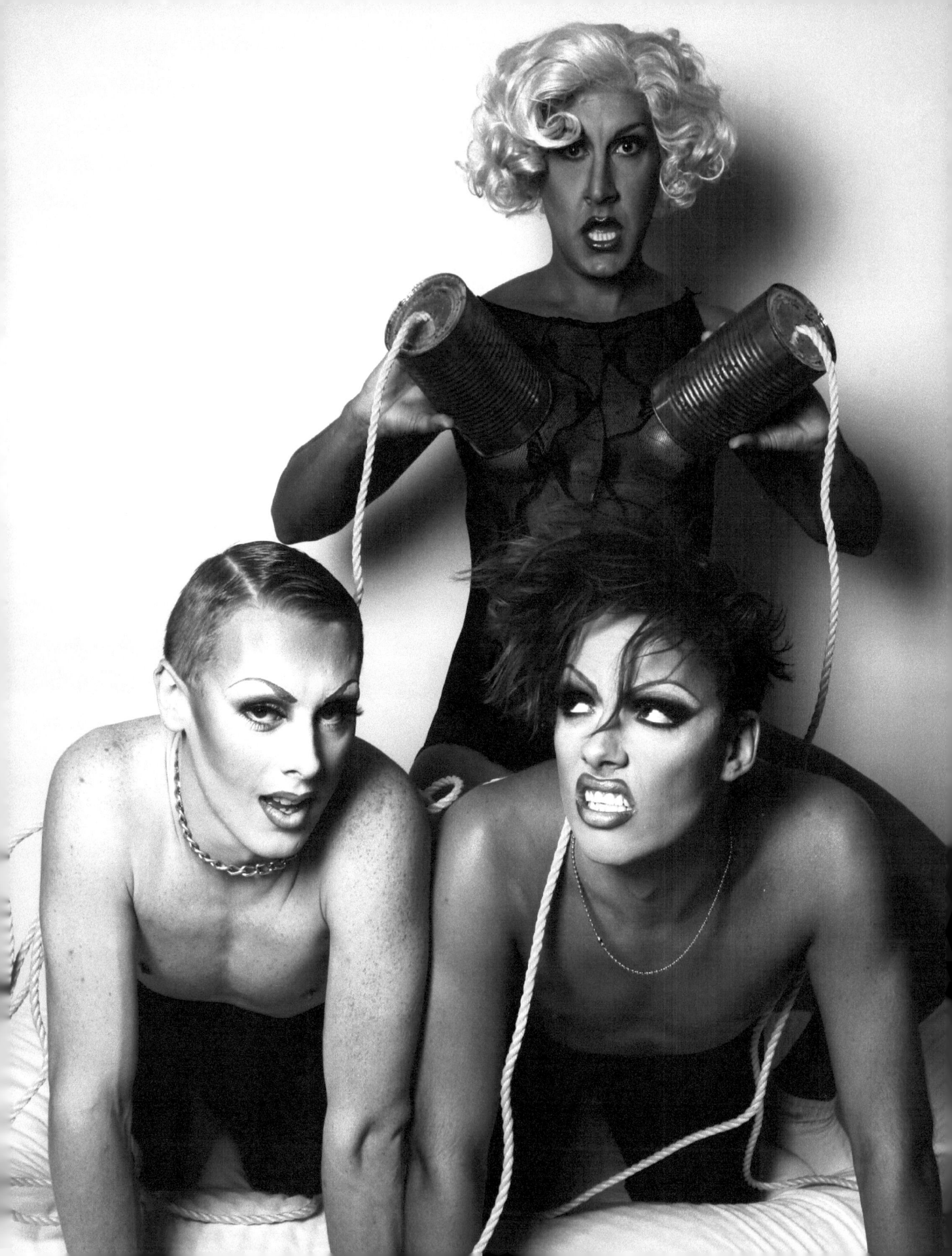

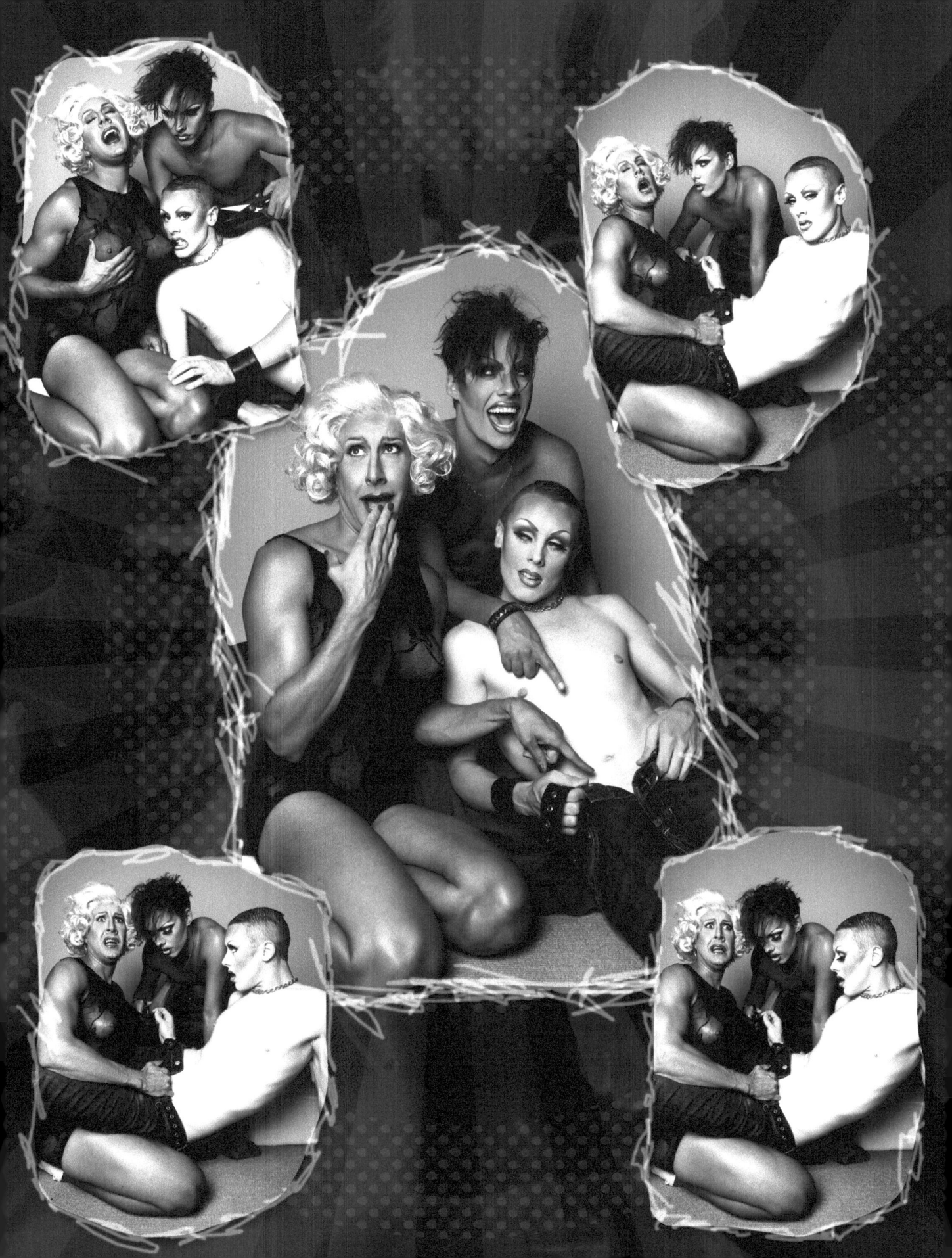

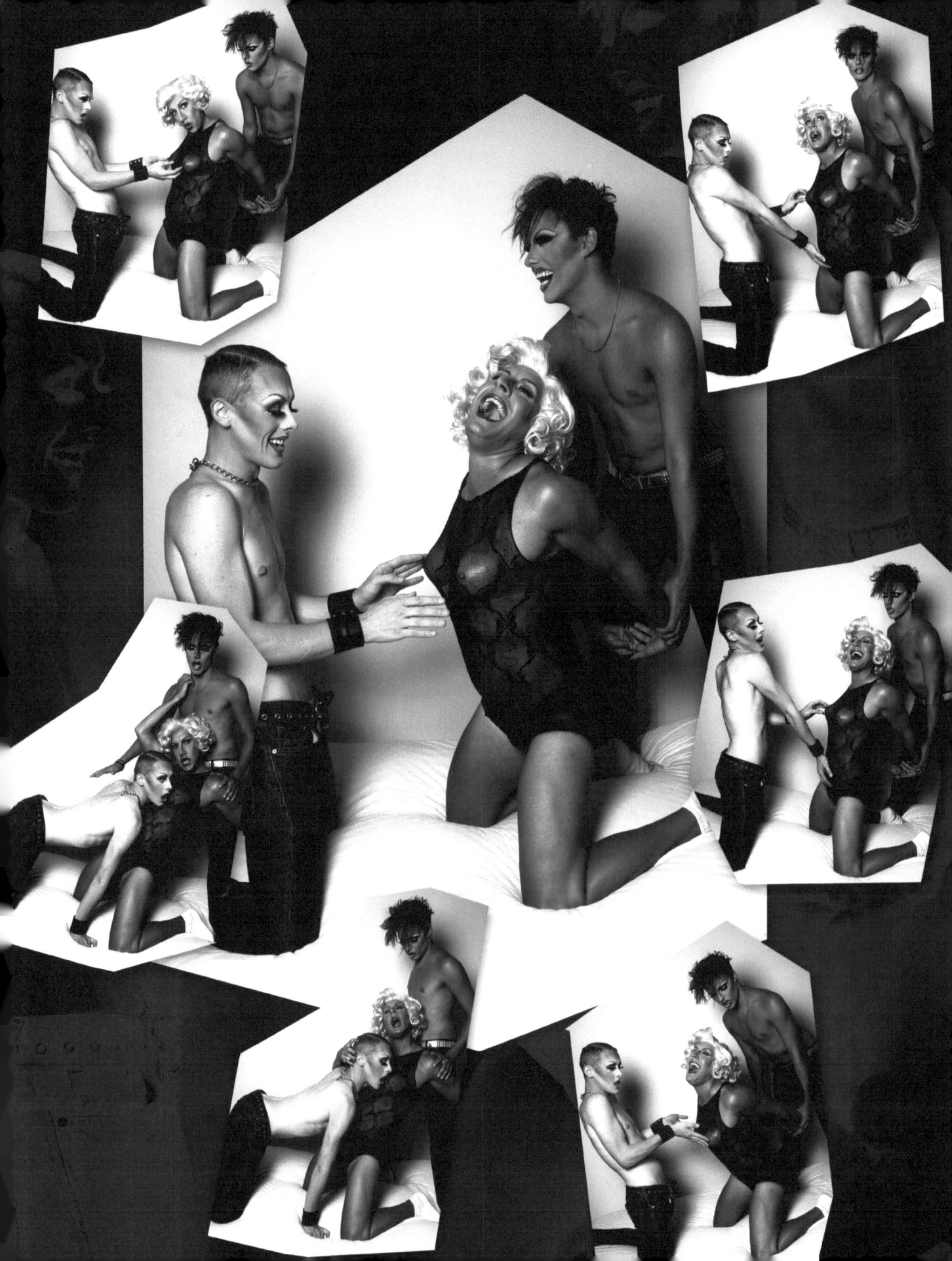

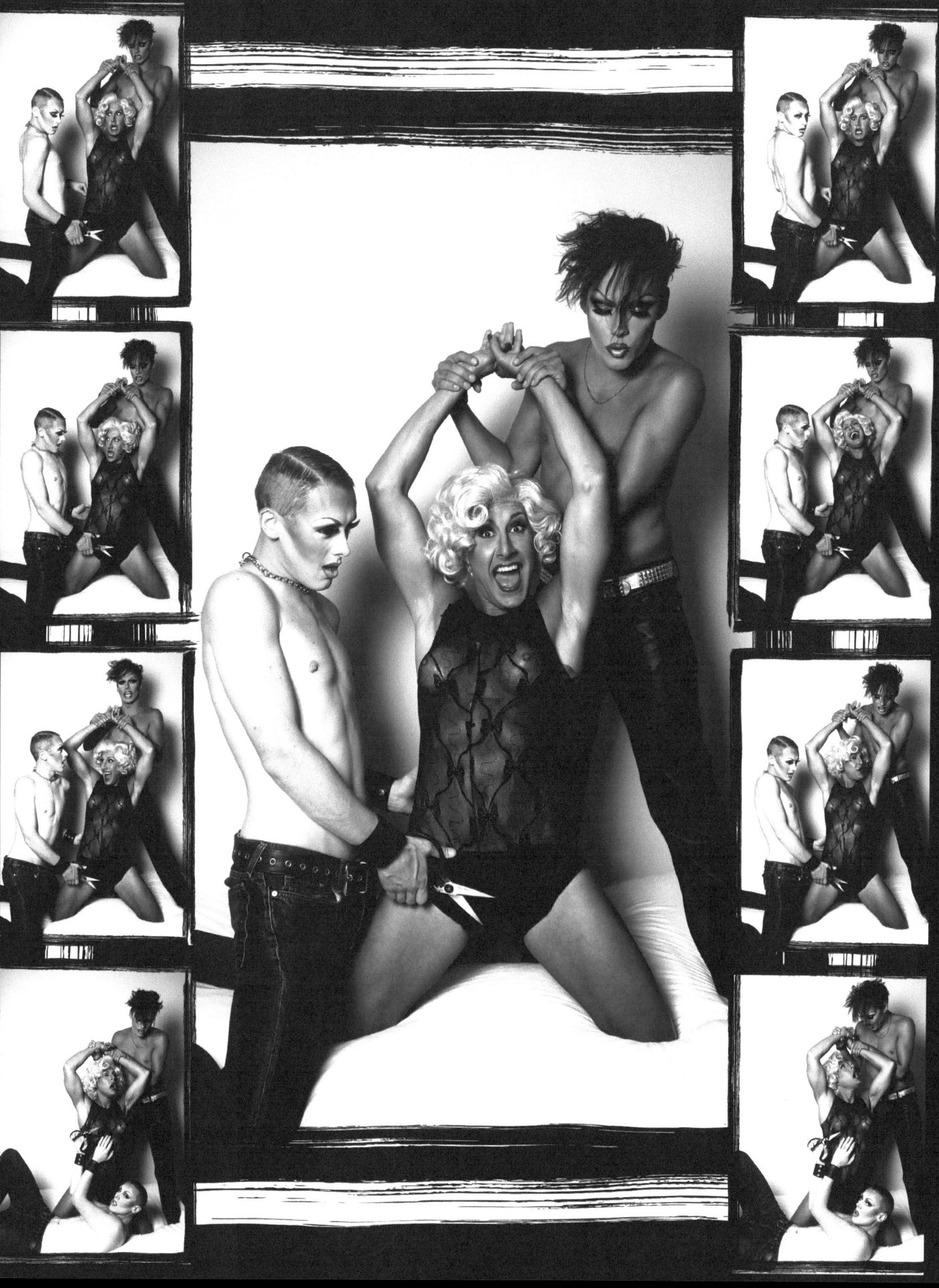

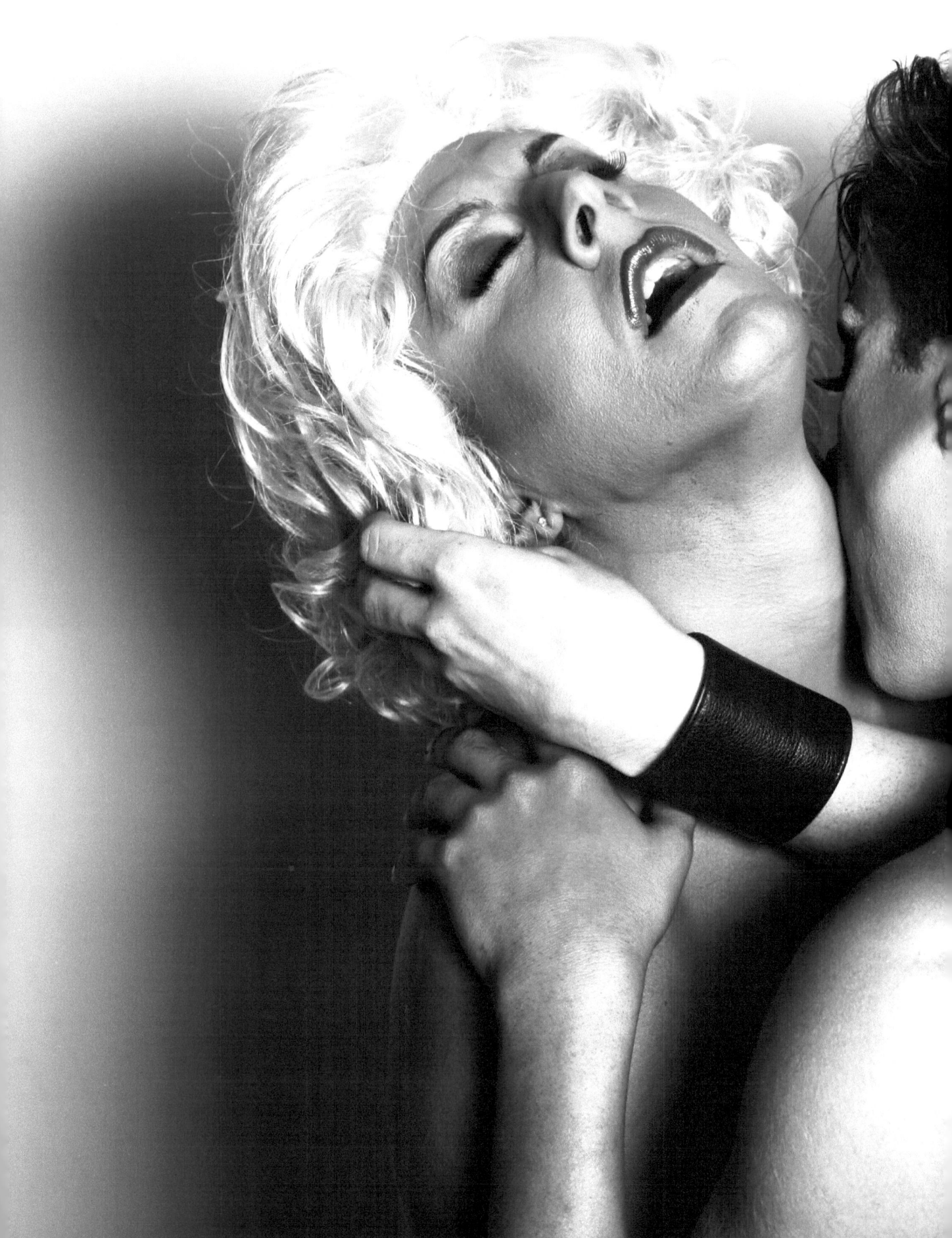

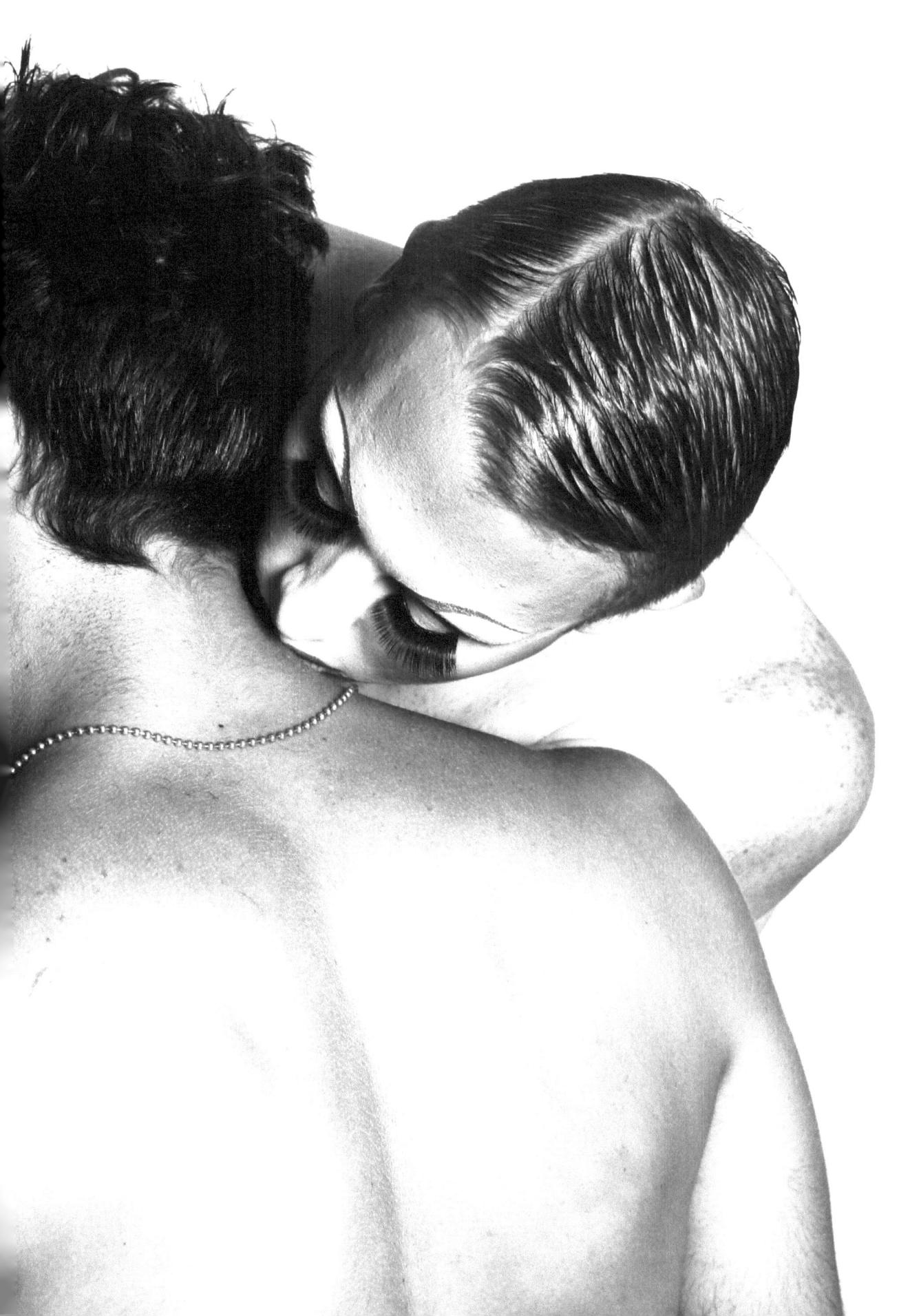

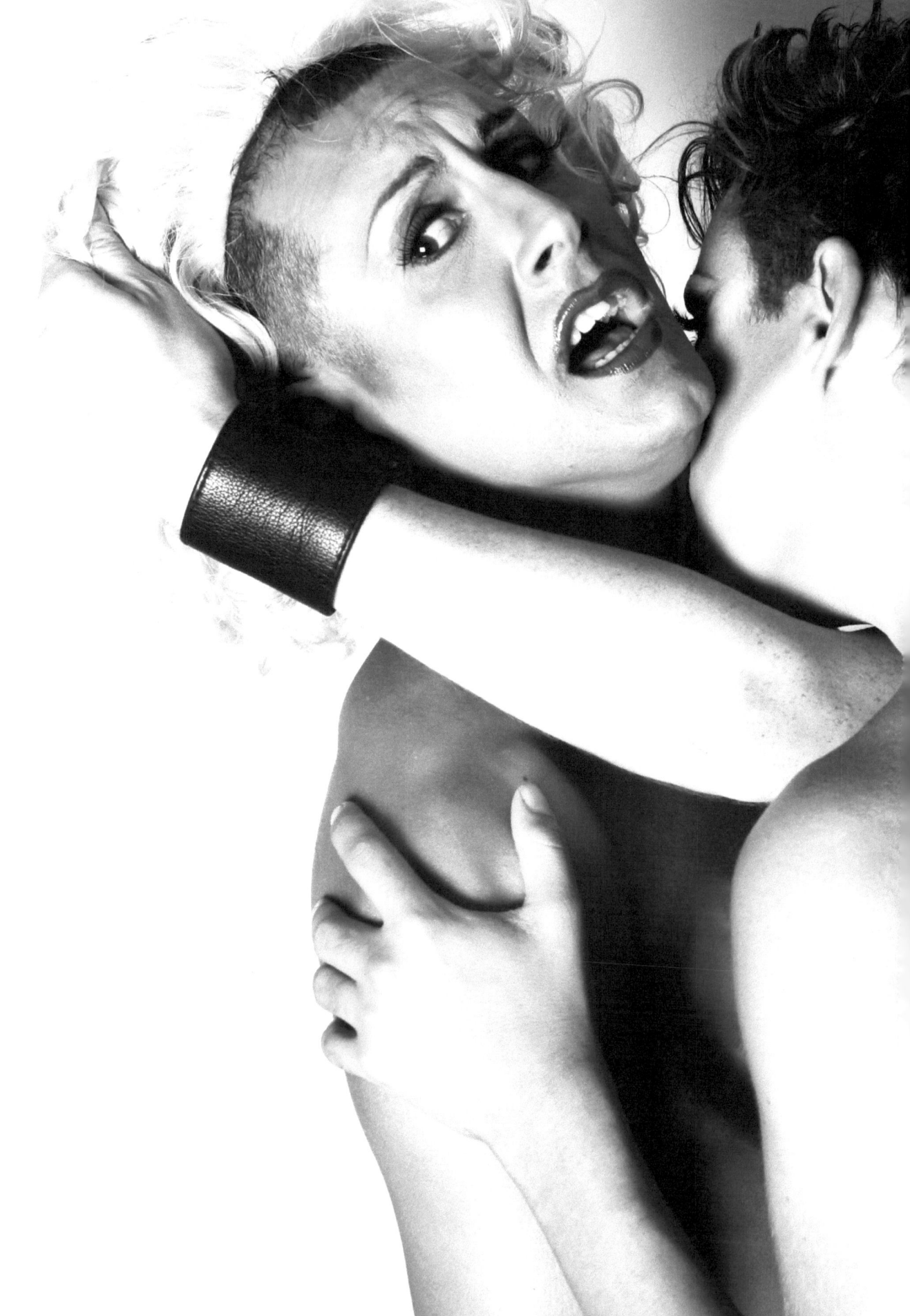

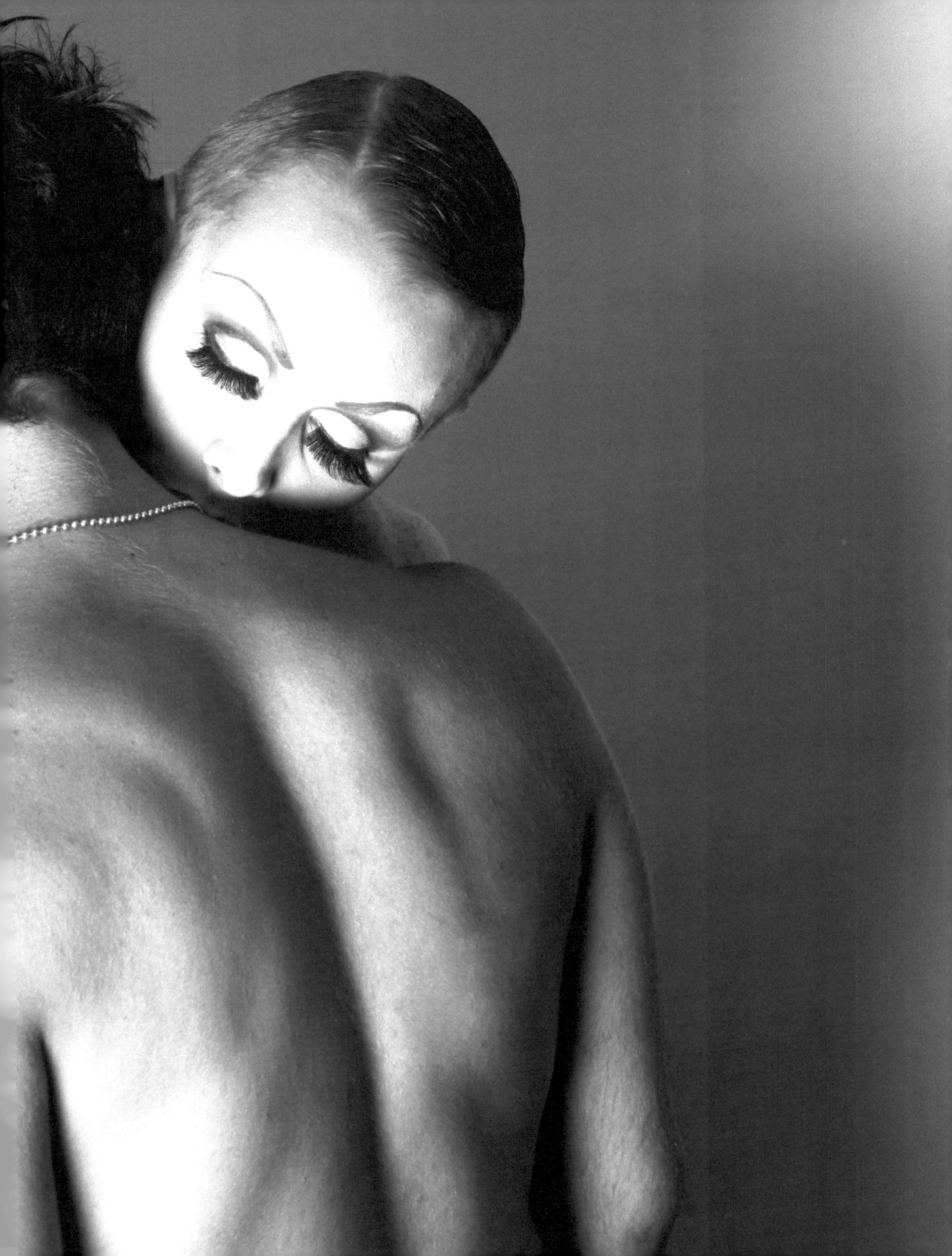

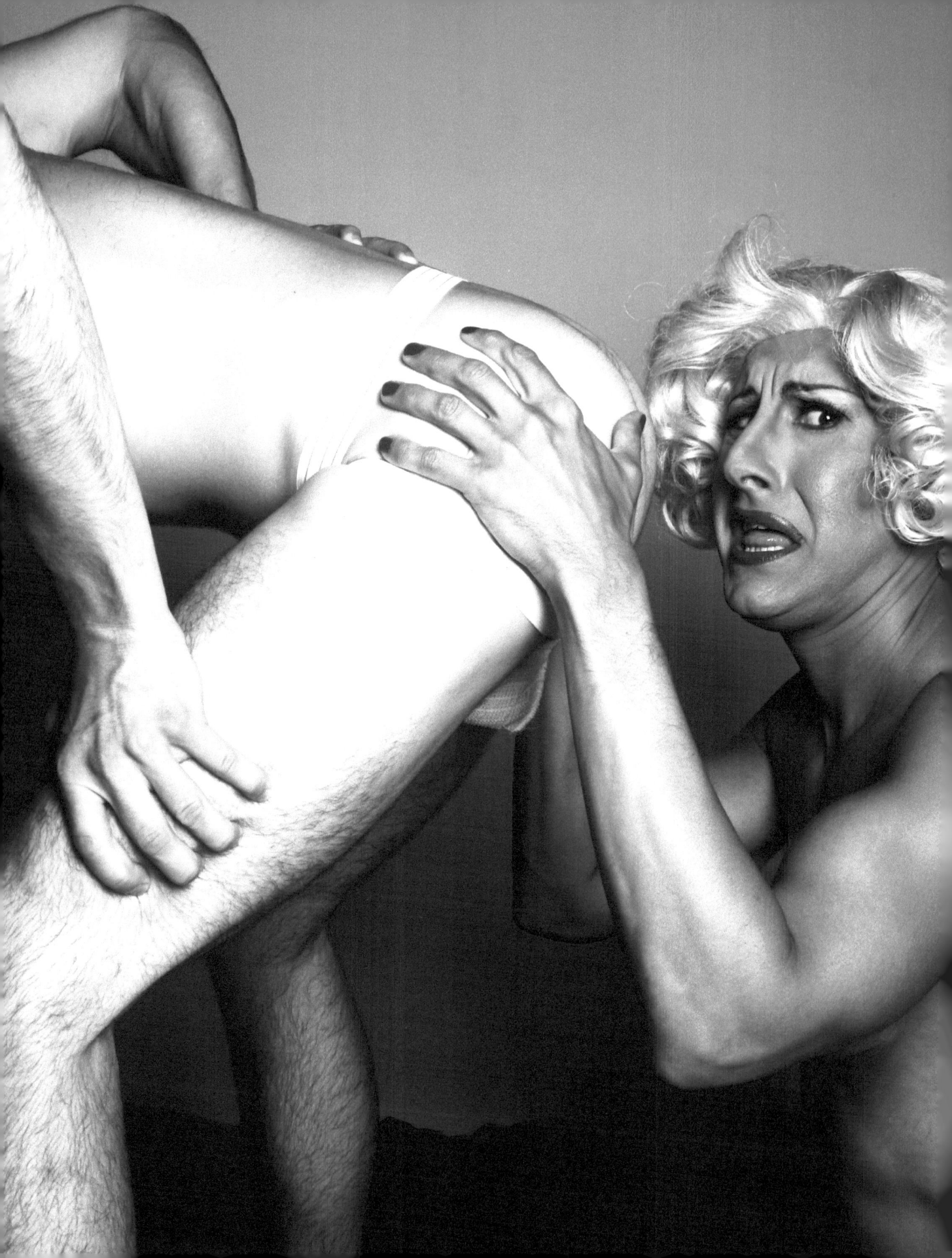

Dear Johnny,

I know I told you I would eat your hole if you got that nasty hair of yours under control, but I just can't. Now before you get mad at me, put yourself in my Payless pumps. I mean, here I am, all ready to ream your rump, only to see a piece of corn sticking out of it! I am just about ready to lose my lunch.

And the stench! Oh, Lord. The stench! Your bunghole seriously smells like one of those homeless people who clear out a subway car. I'm not exaggerating. You need to take a long hot shower. And use soap. And scrub. And rinse. And repeat.

- Chita.

PS: Spray with bleach if necessary.

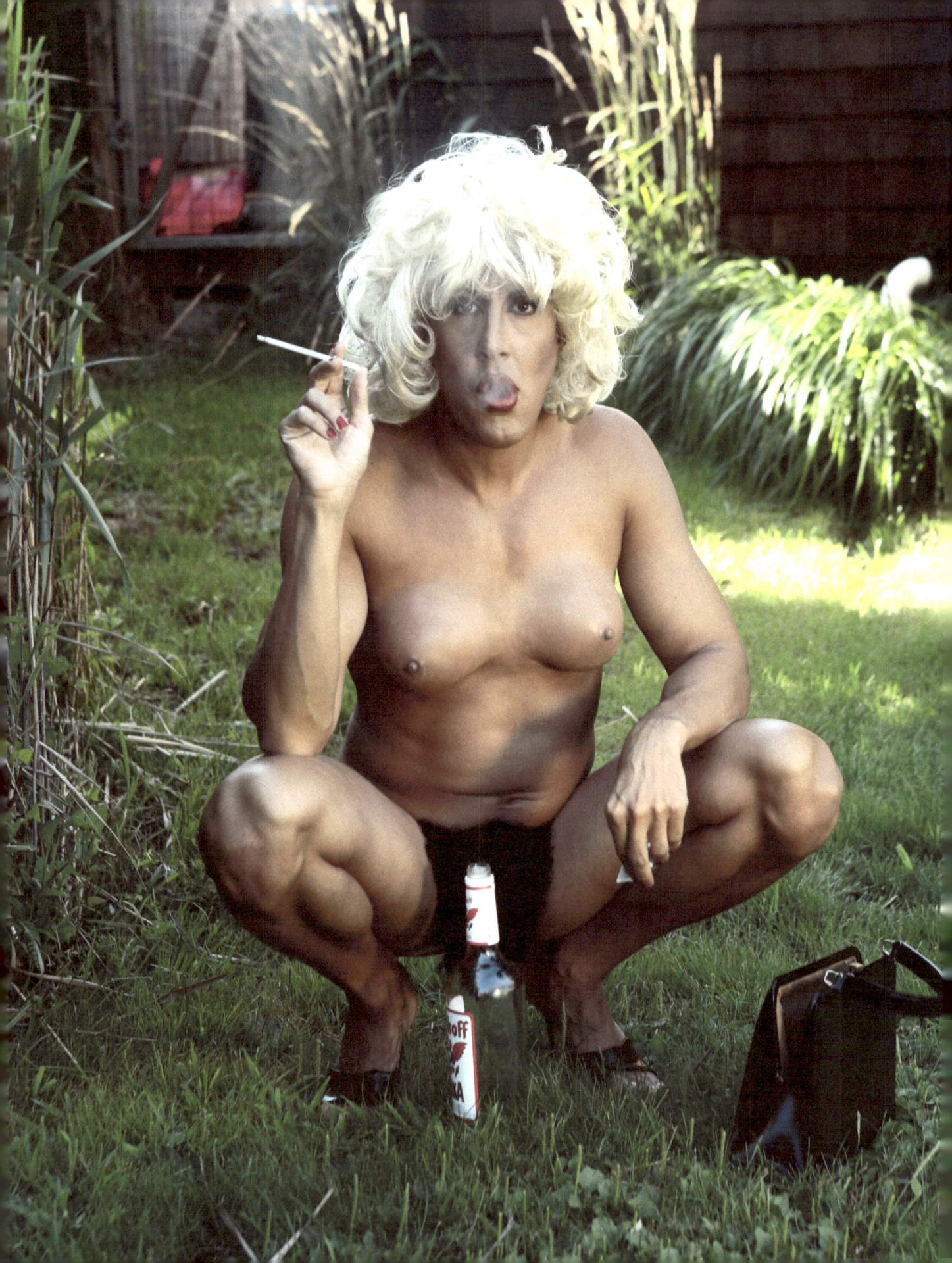

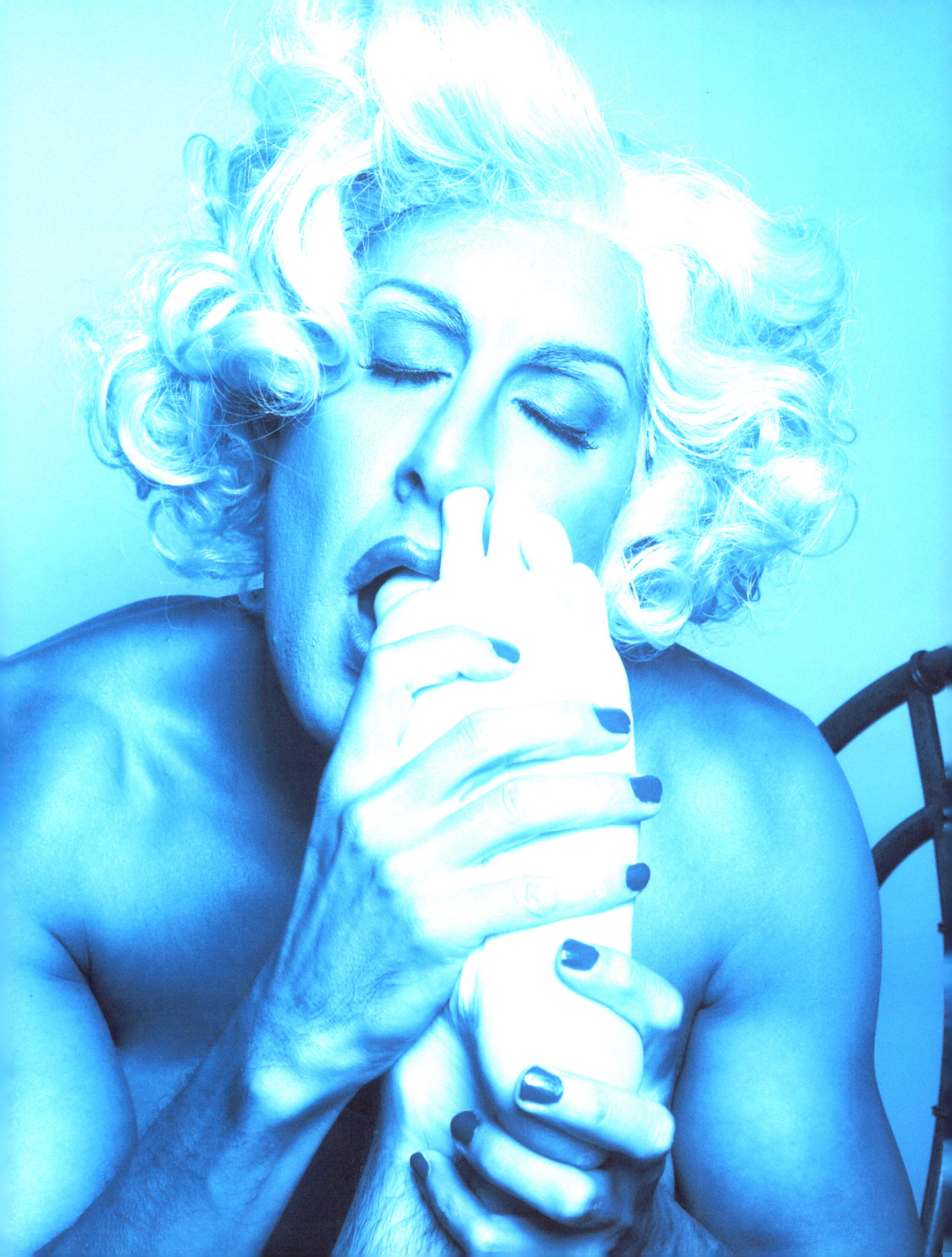

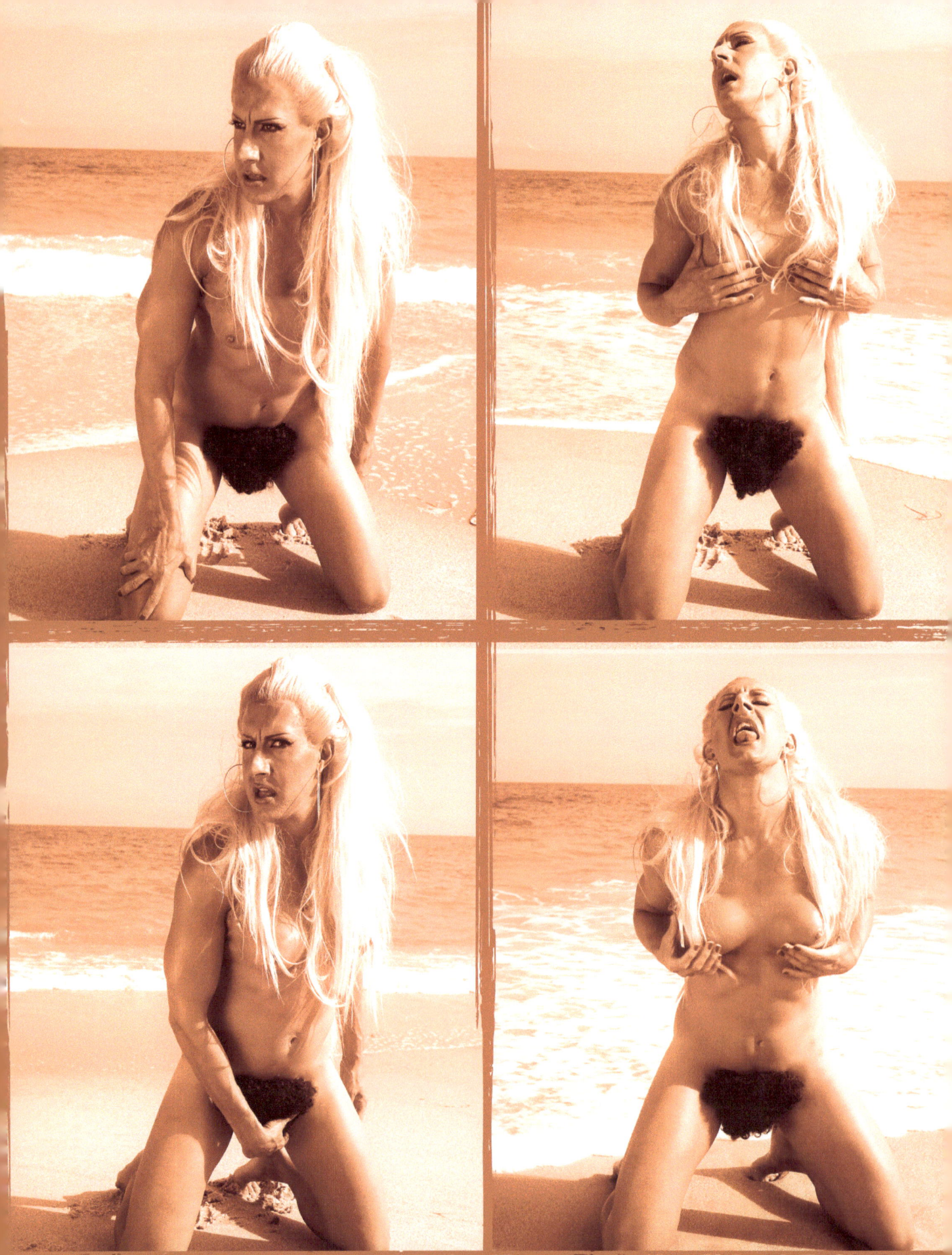

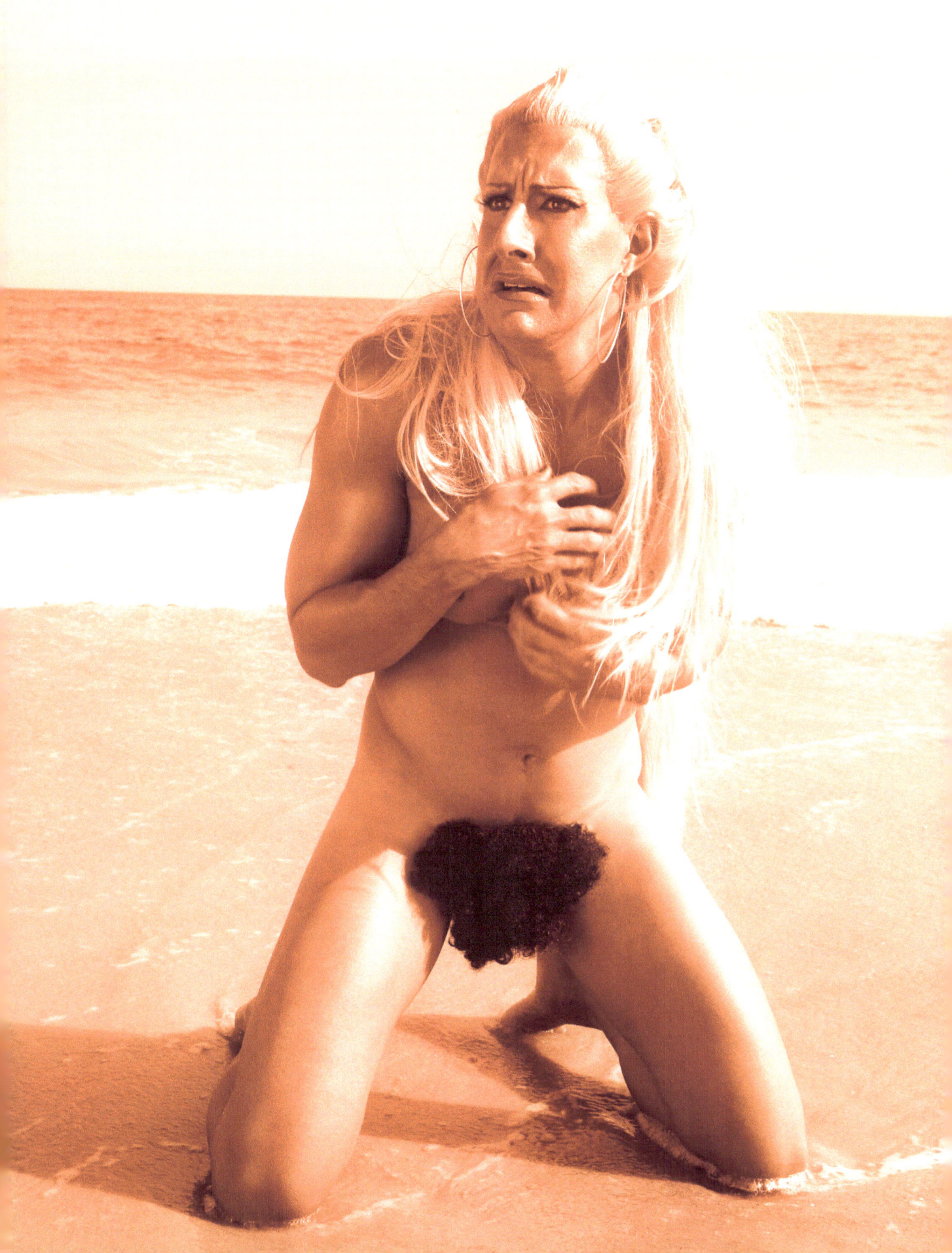

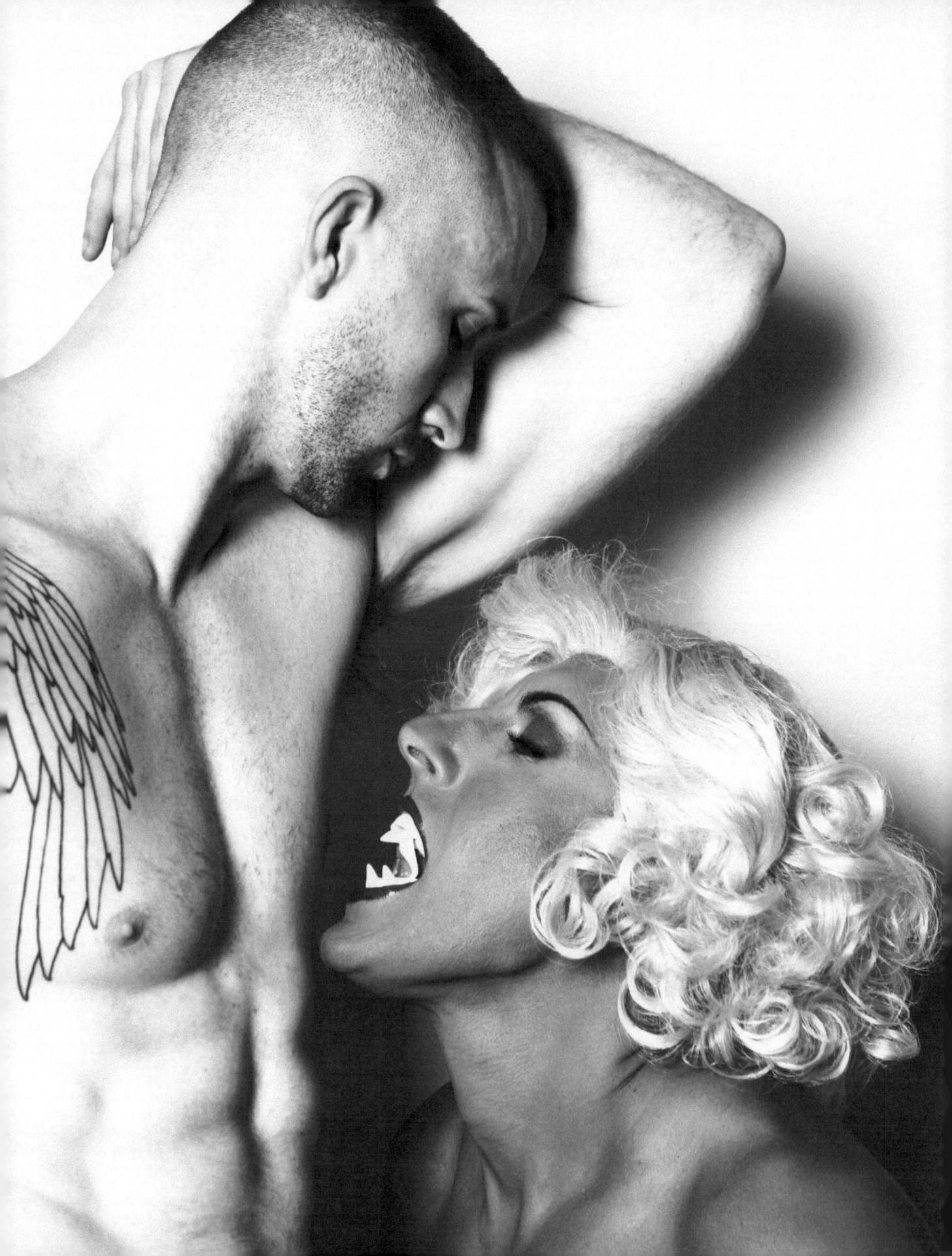

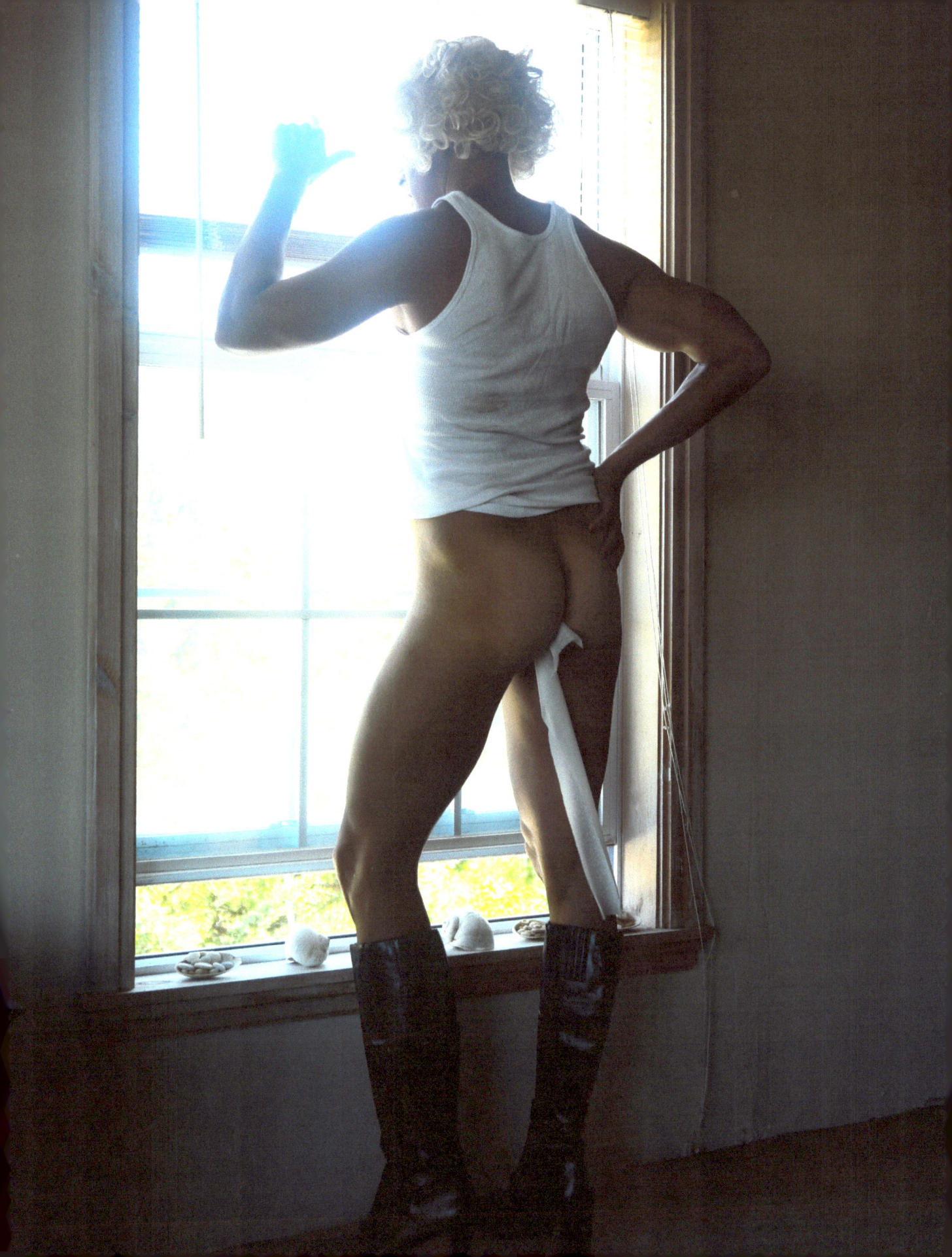

I like my pussy. Sometimes I stare at it in the mirror, thinking, "How the fuck did I get a pussy? I'm a man." But then I look at it again and realize it's actually a penis and then I'm like, "God, that has to be the smallest penis in the world! It's basically like an enlarged clit!!" And then I realize I'm actually looking at a hemmorhoid hanging out of my ass. Then I say to myself, "Get yourself to a doctor, QUICK, and STOP EATING THAT KFC! It's wreaking havoc on your digestive tract.

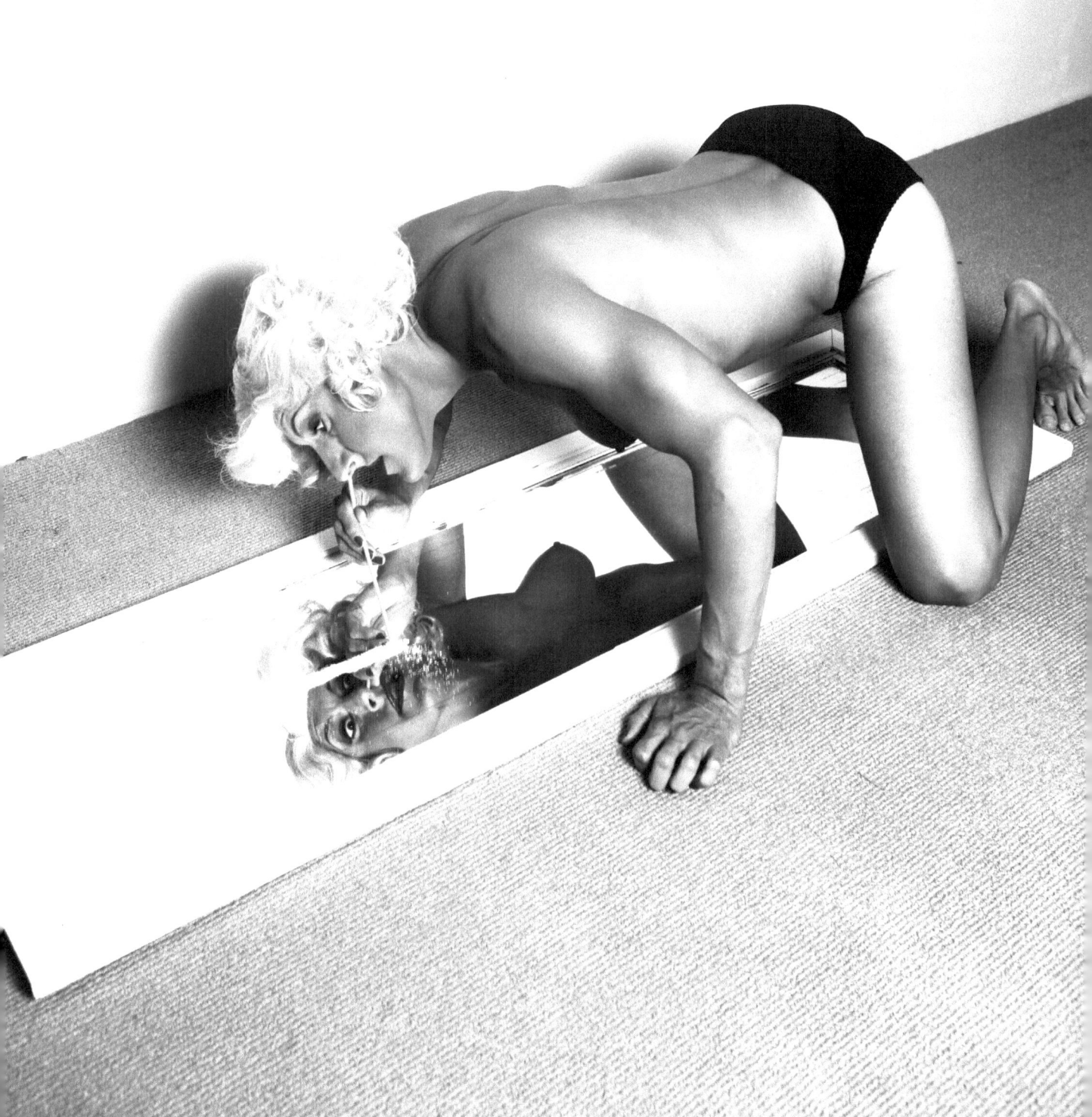

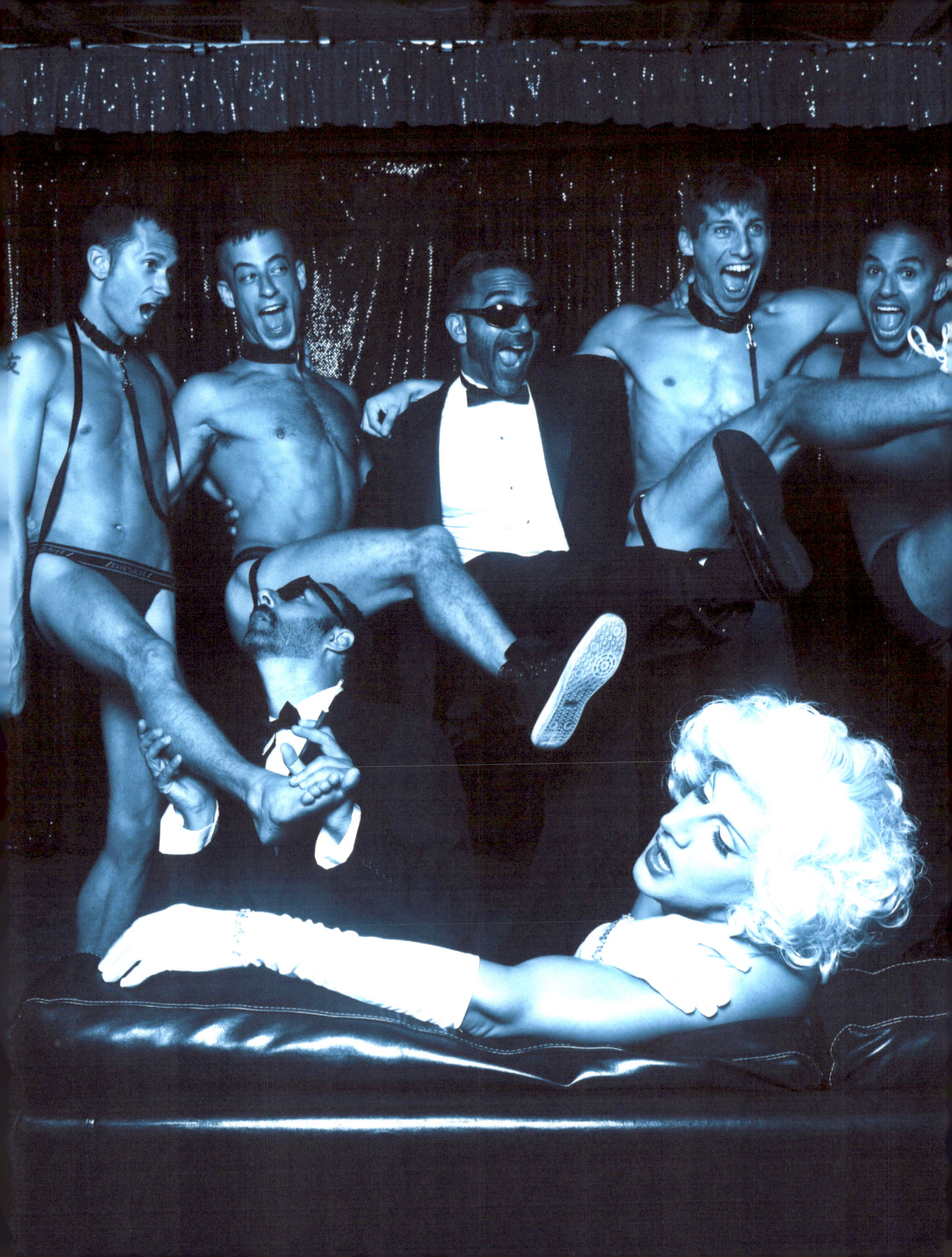

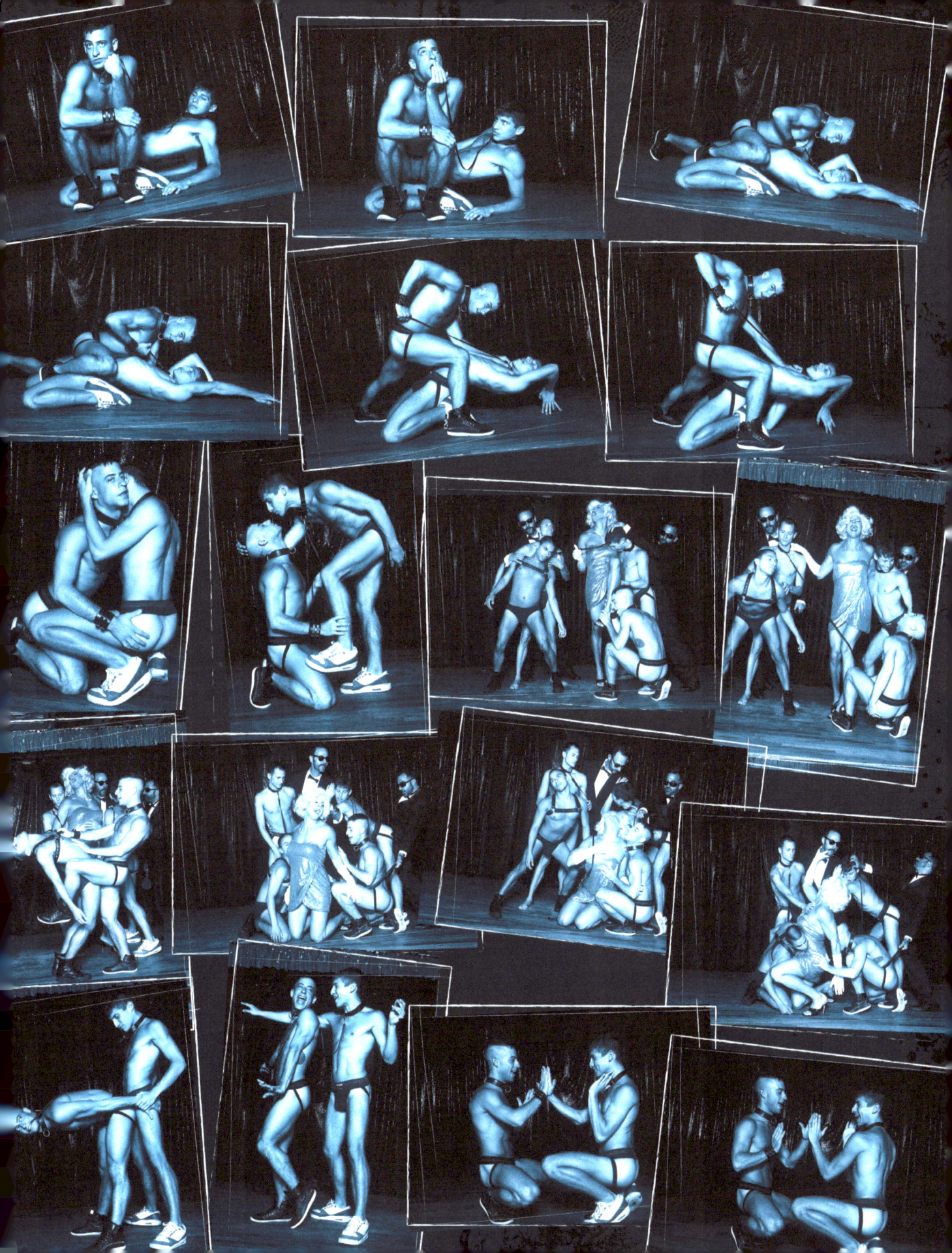

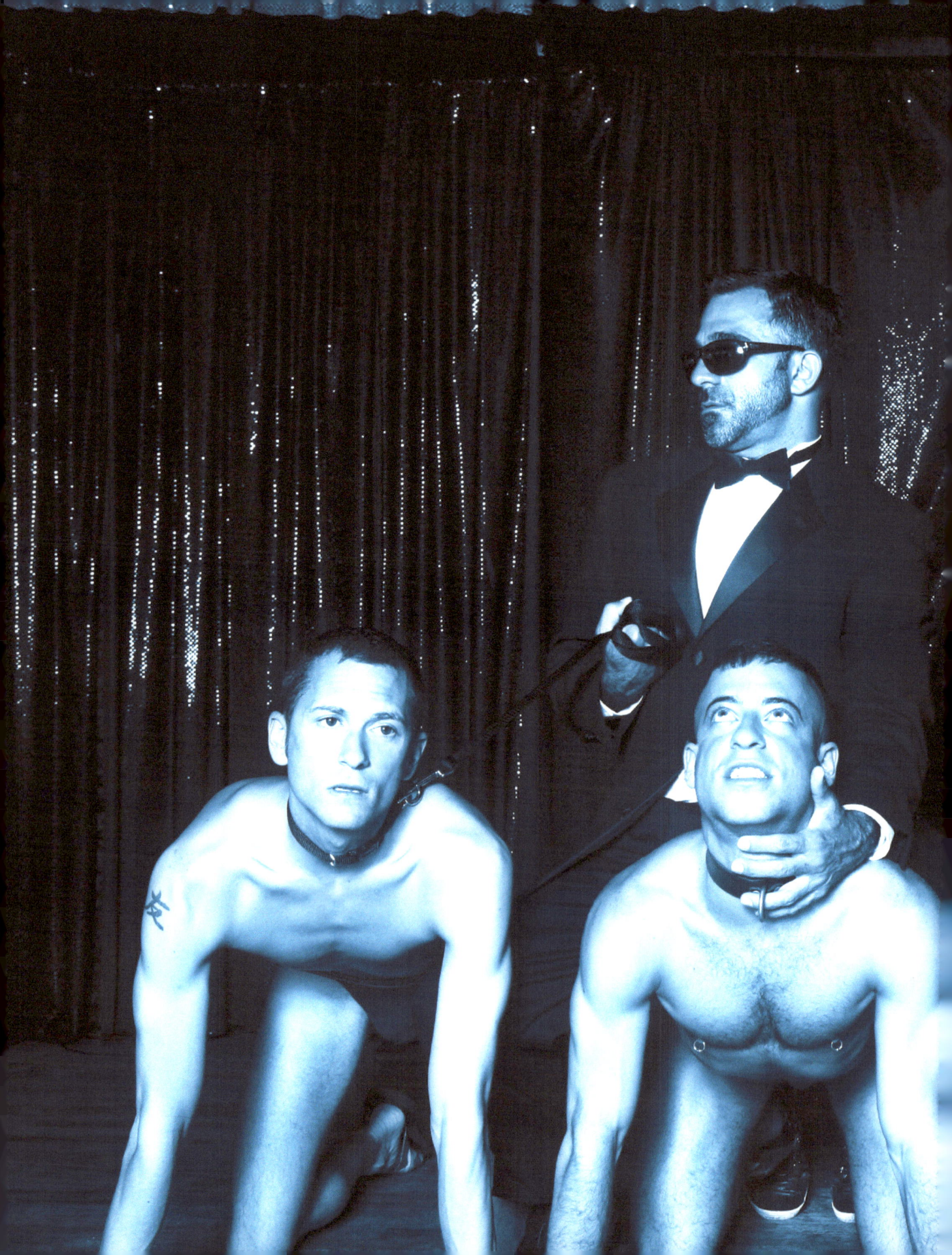

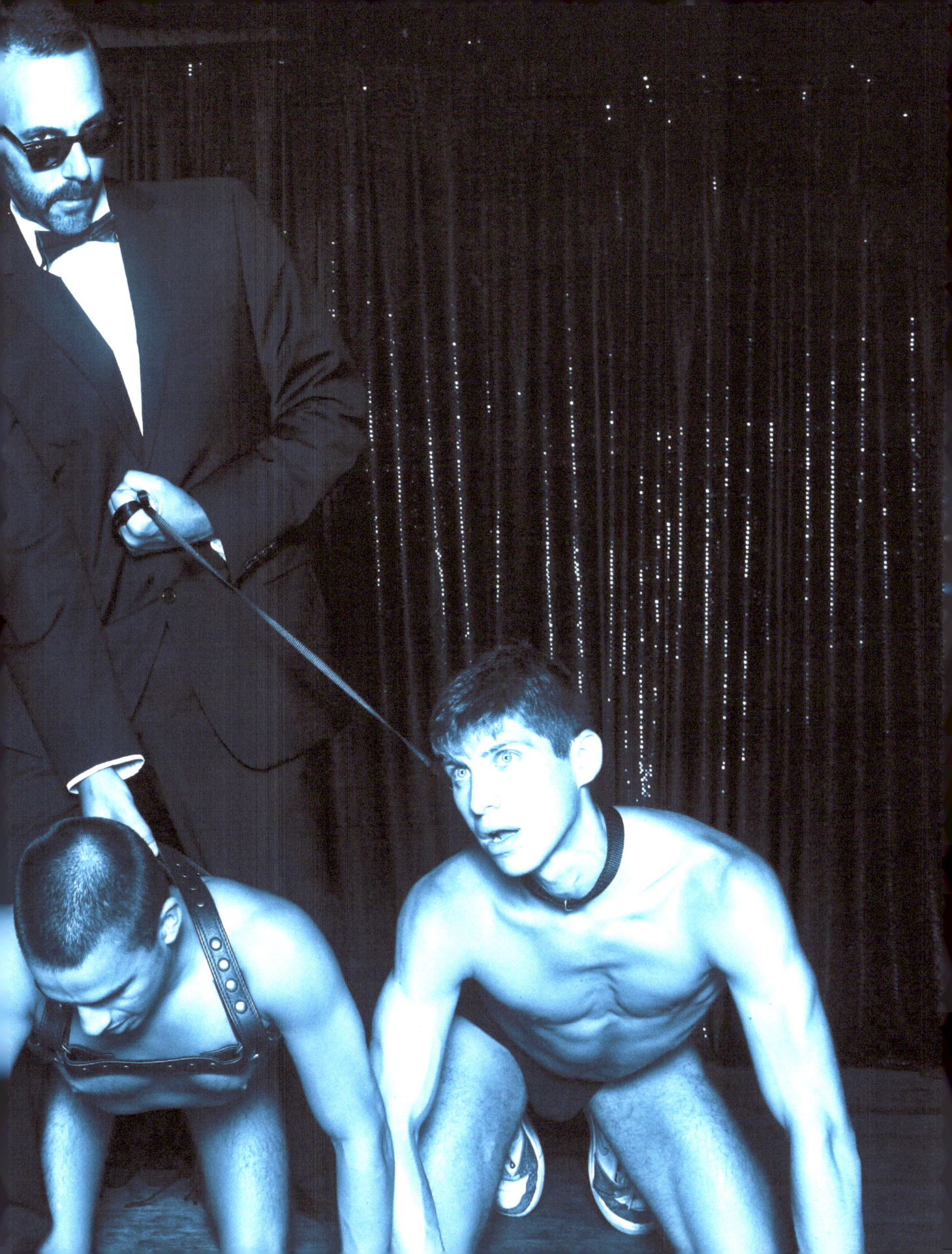

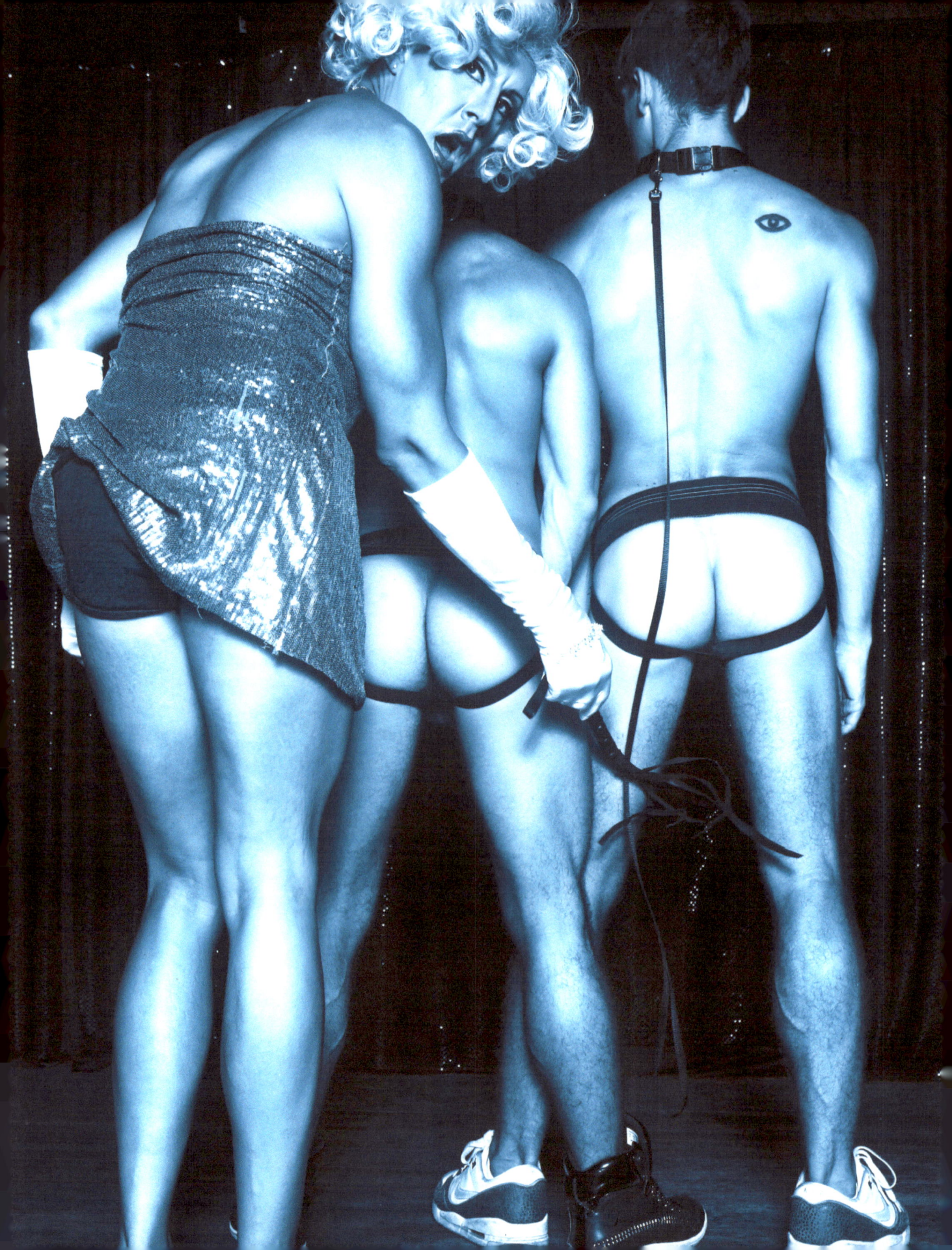

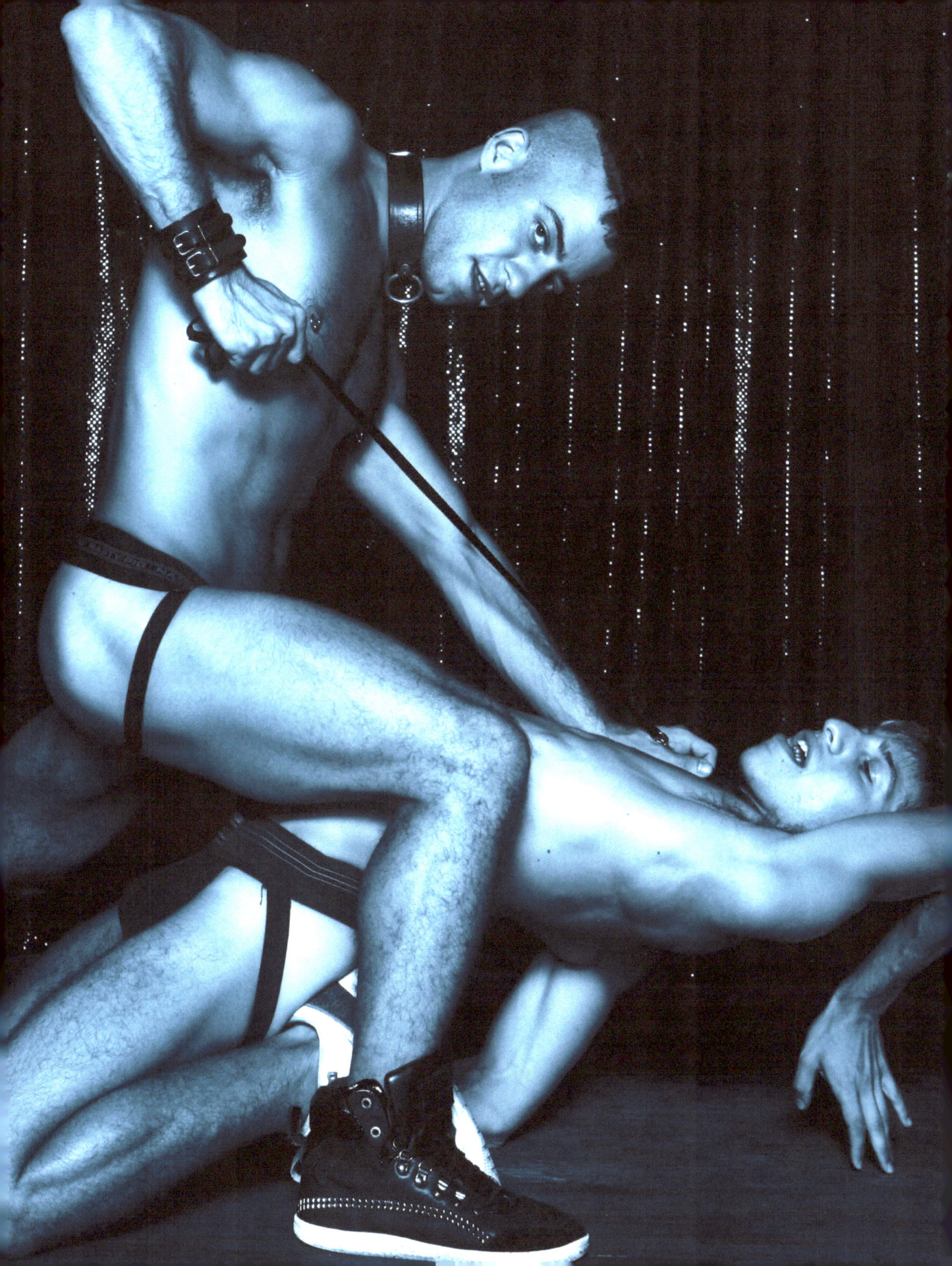

Only the one who hurts you can comfort you. Only the one who inflicts the pain can expect to get they ass whooped. Bitch, I will cut you!

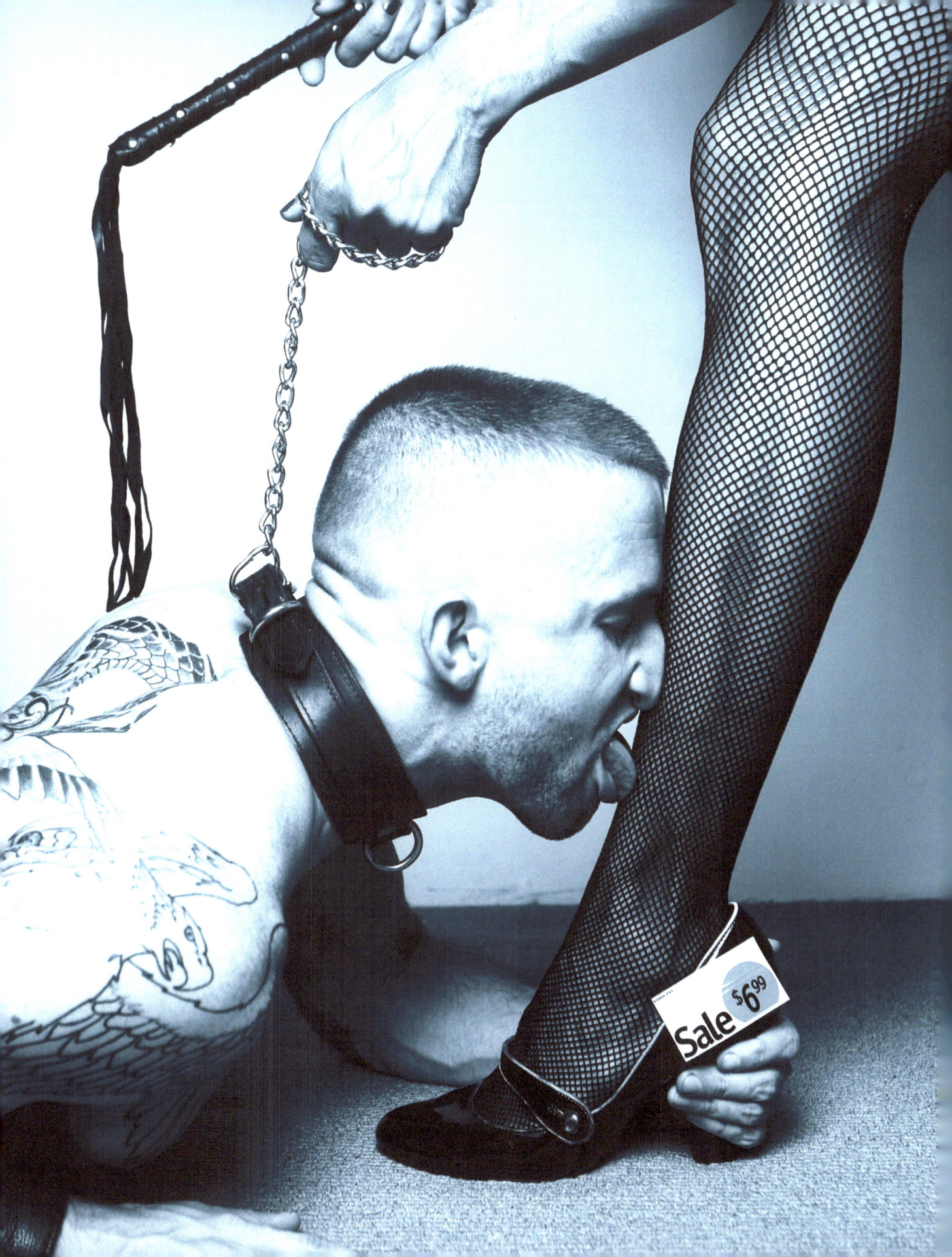

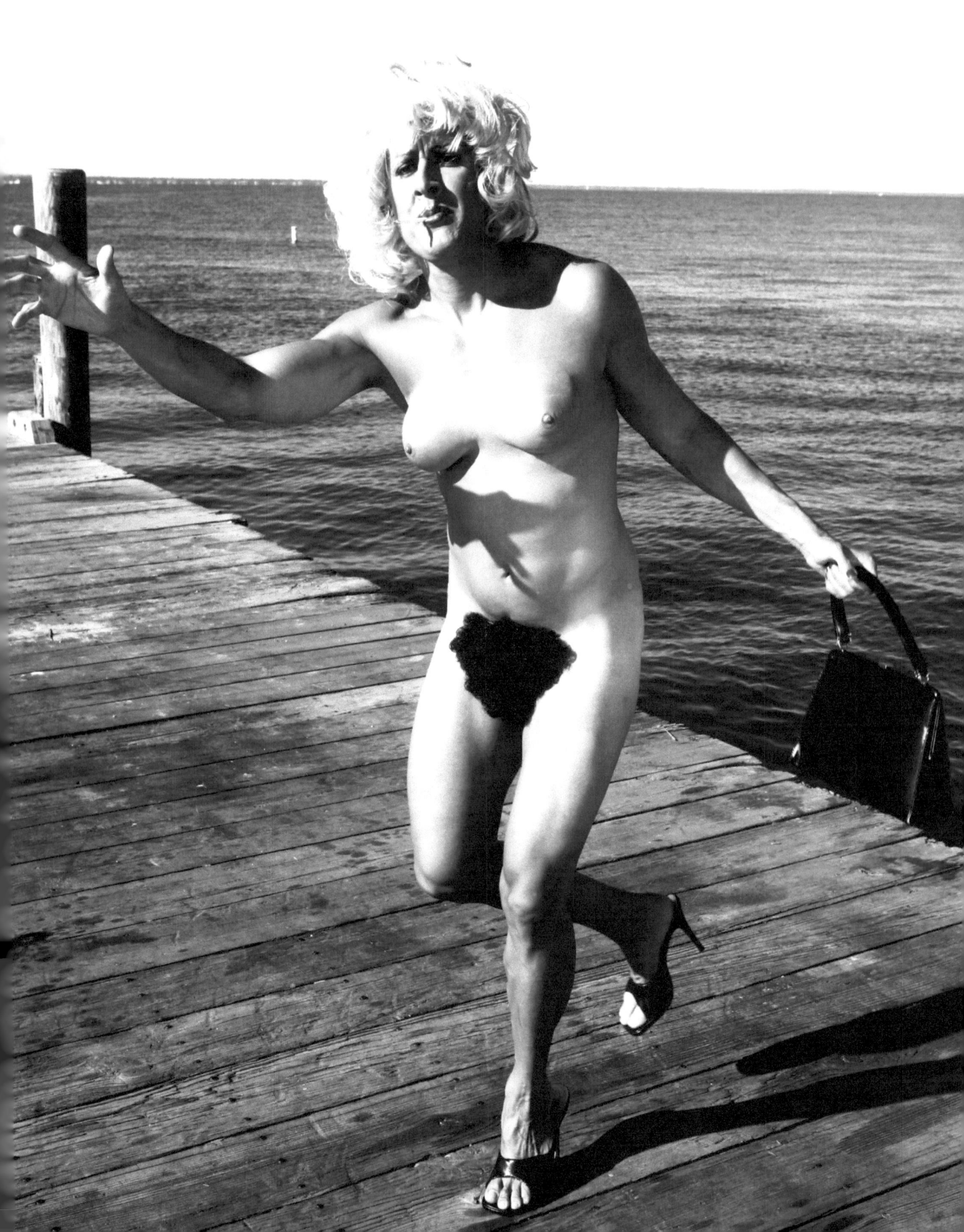

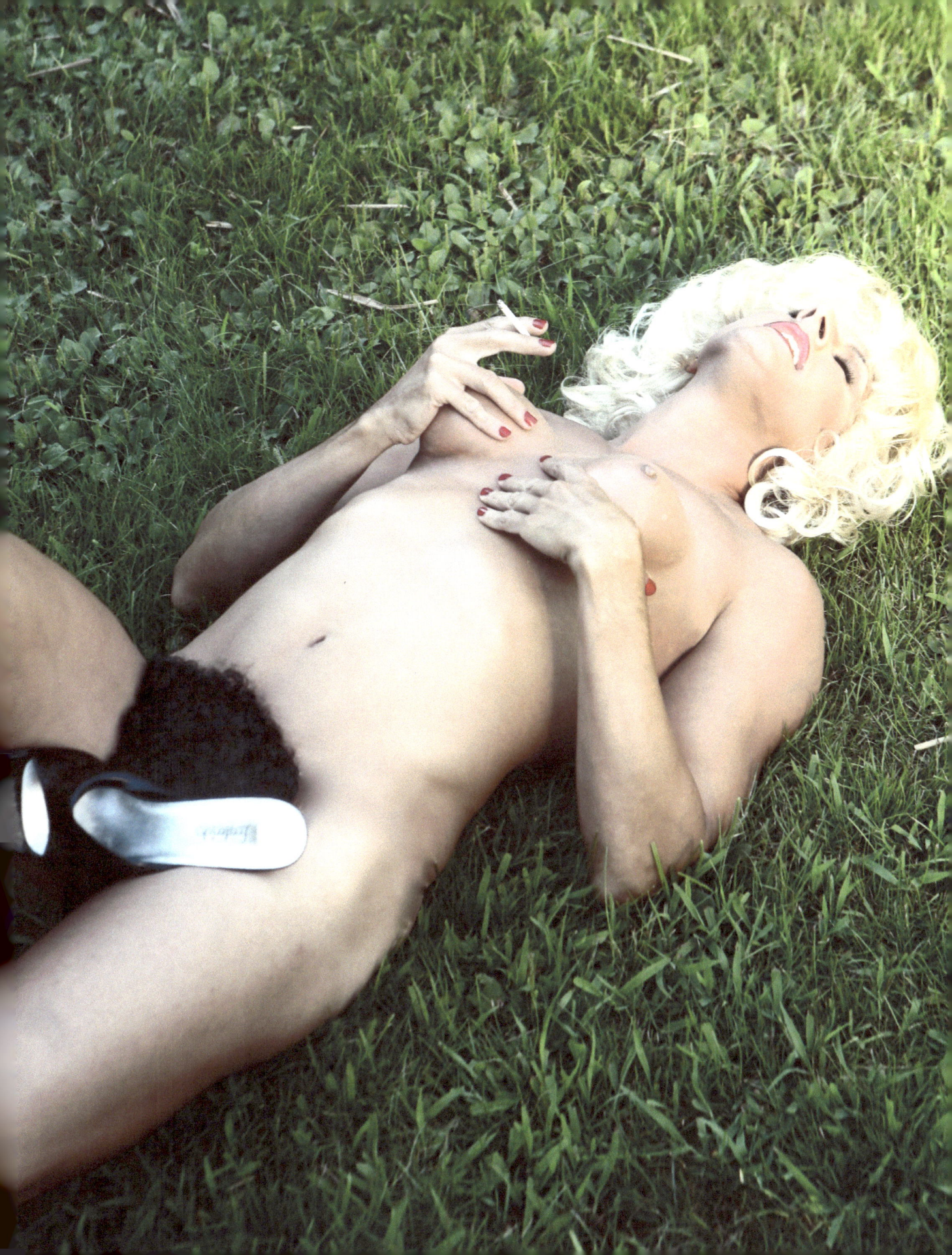

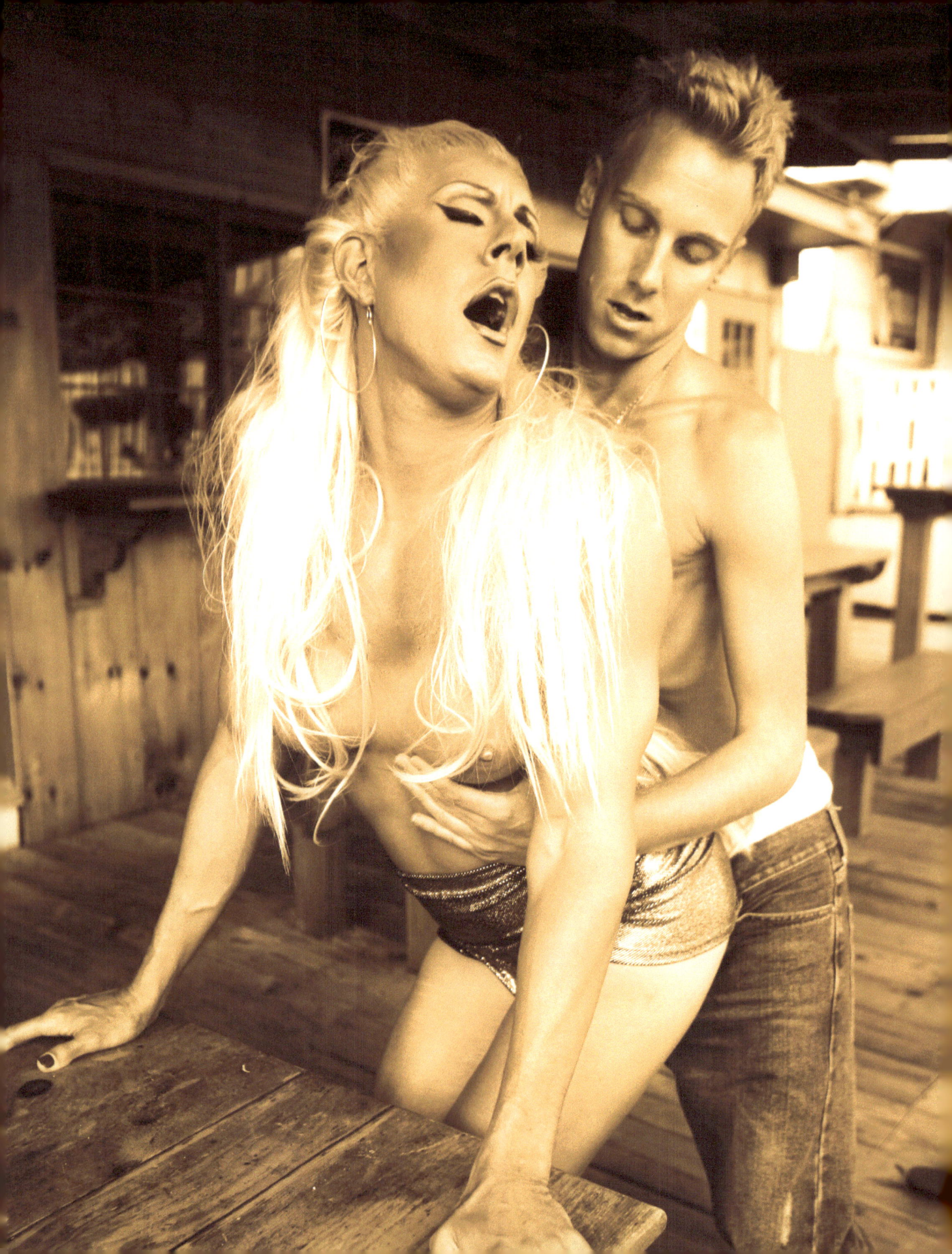

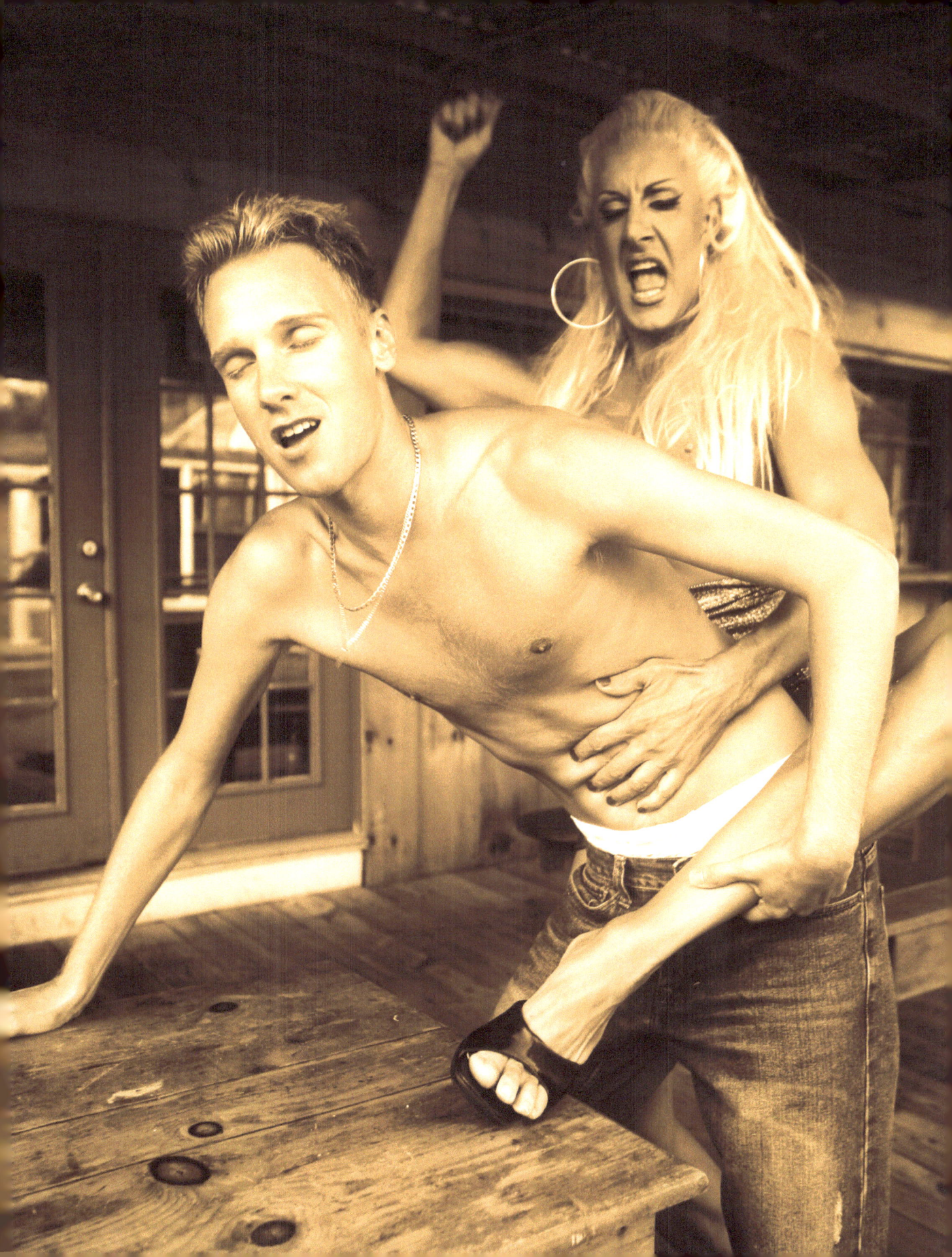

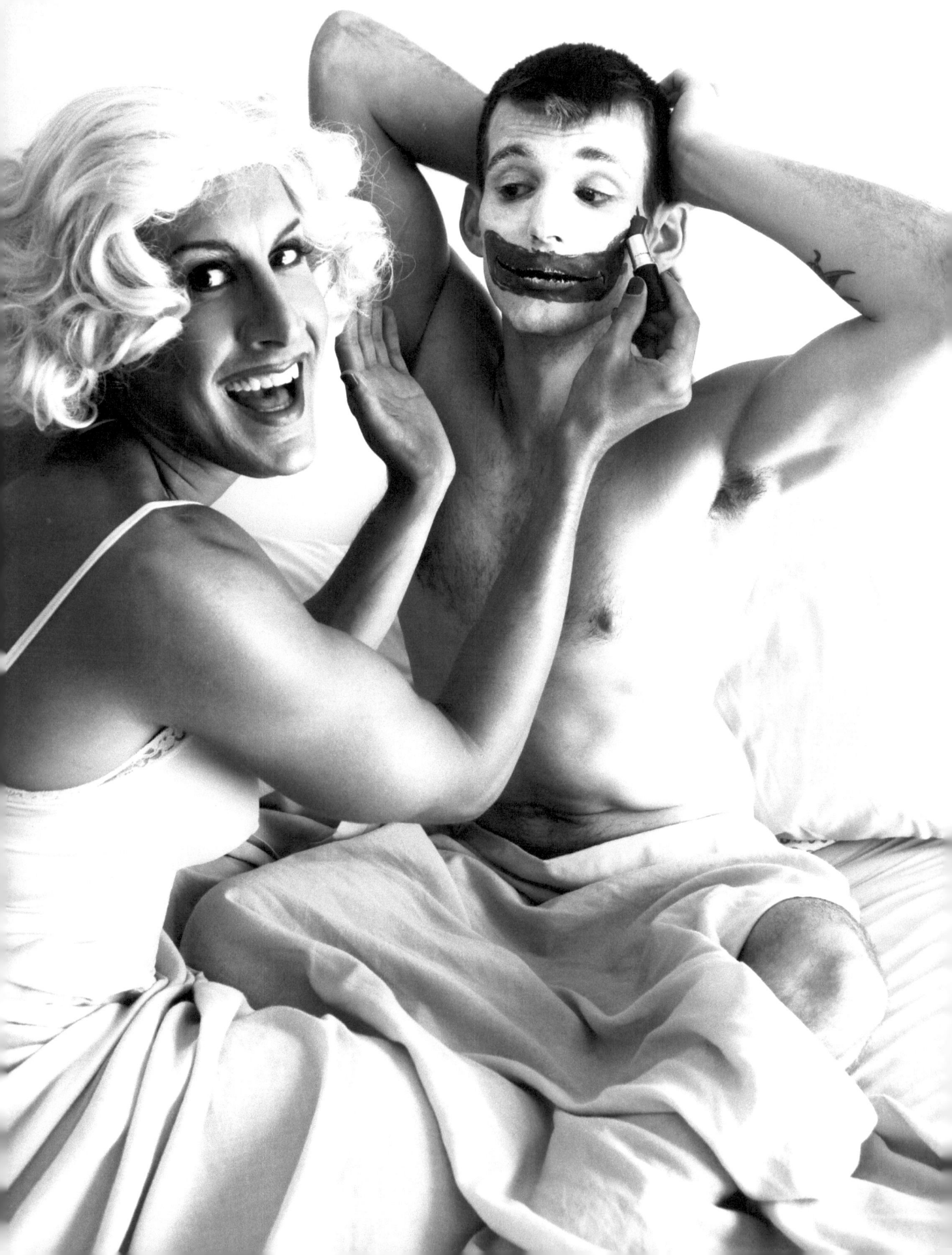

who doesn't love makeup sex?

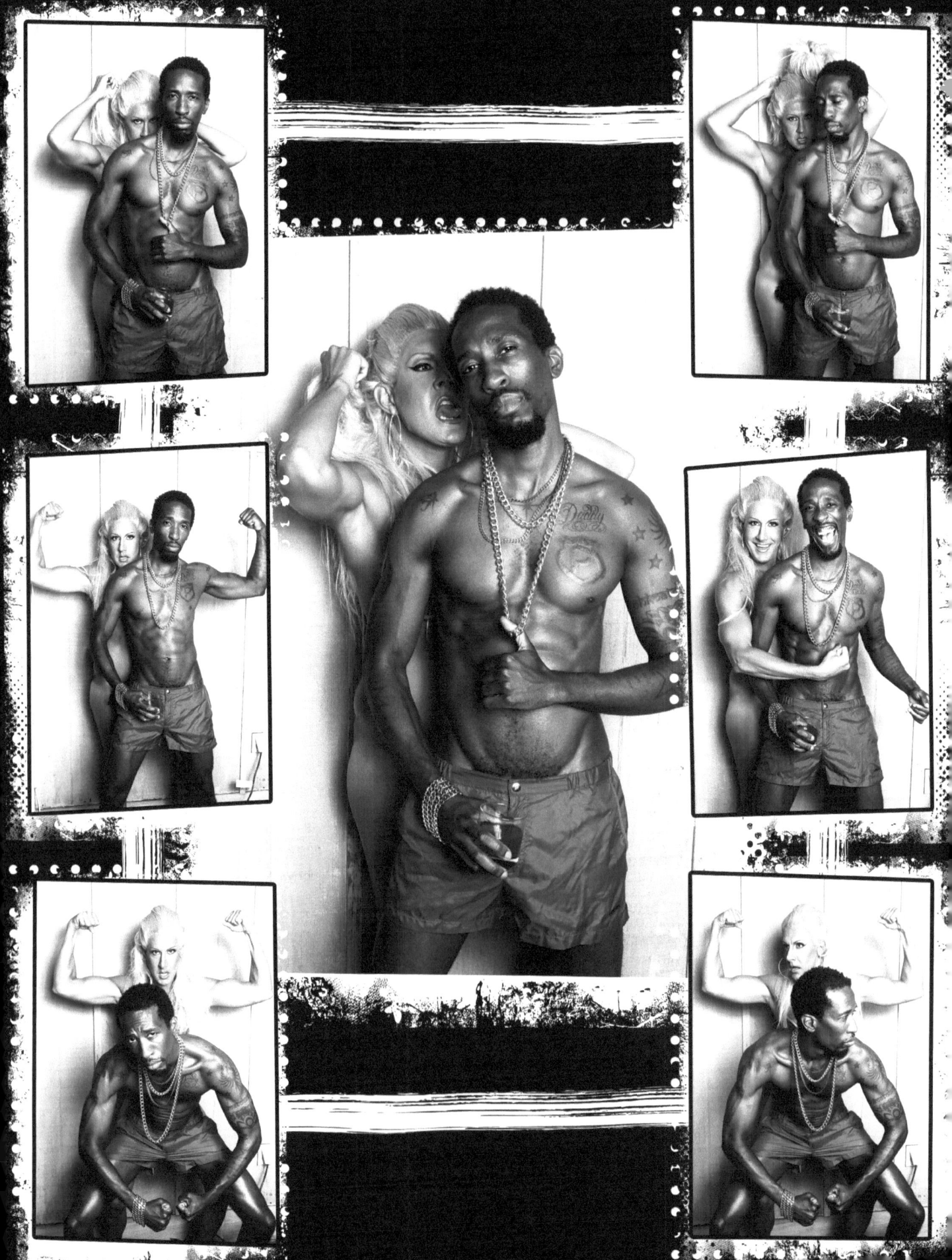

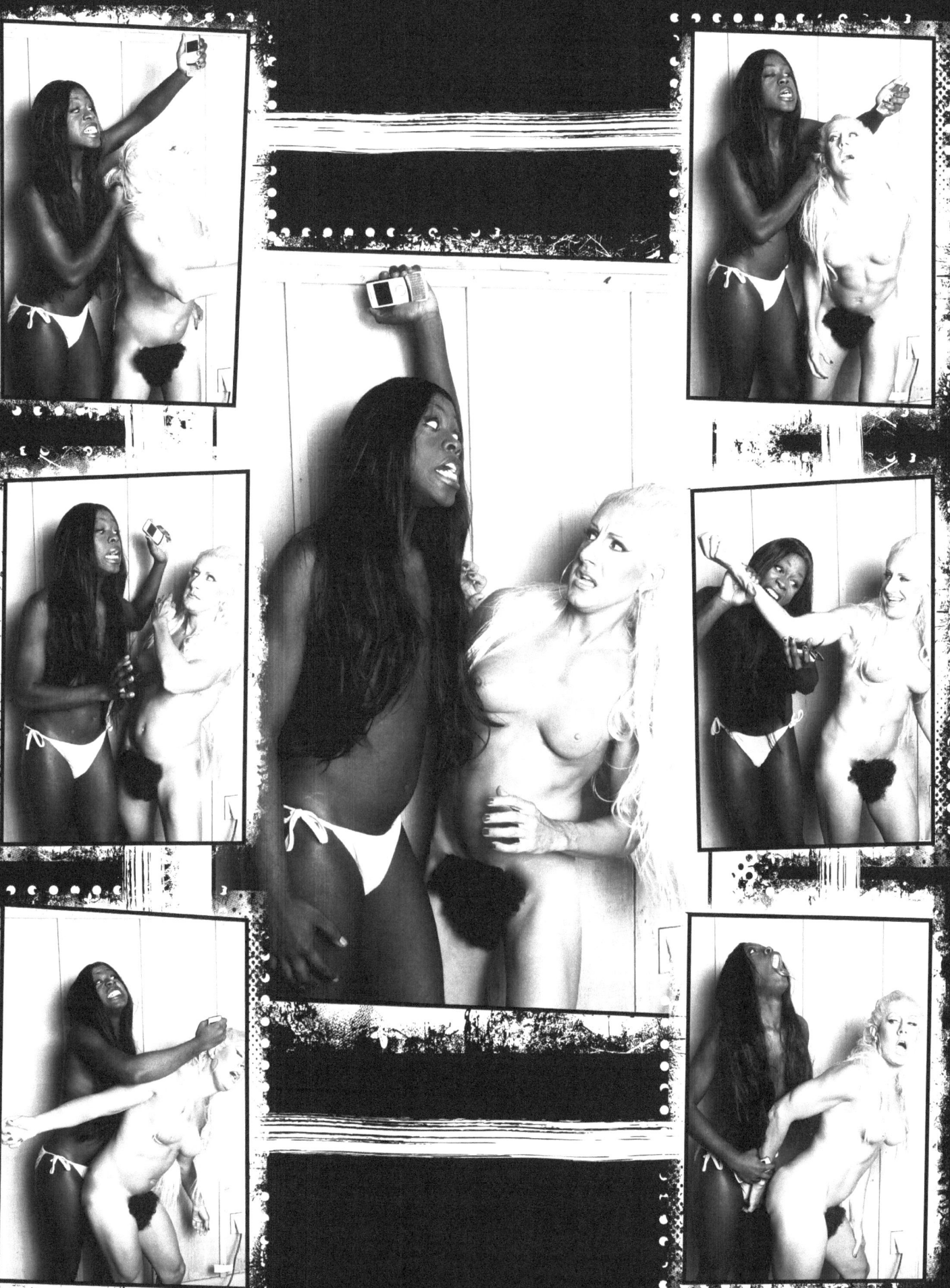

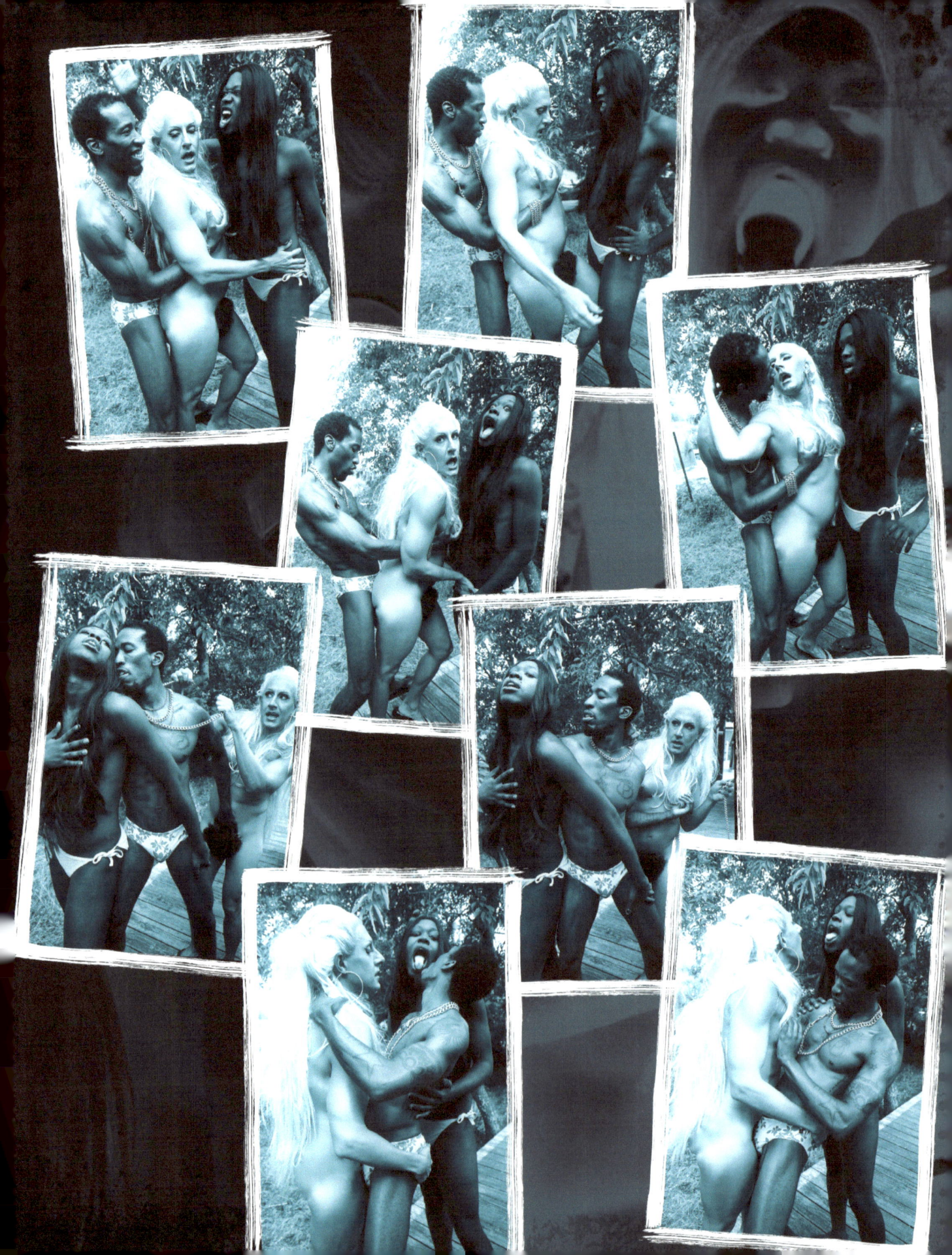

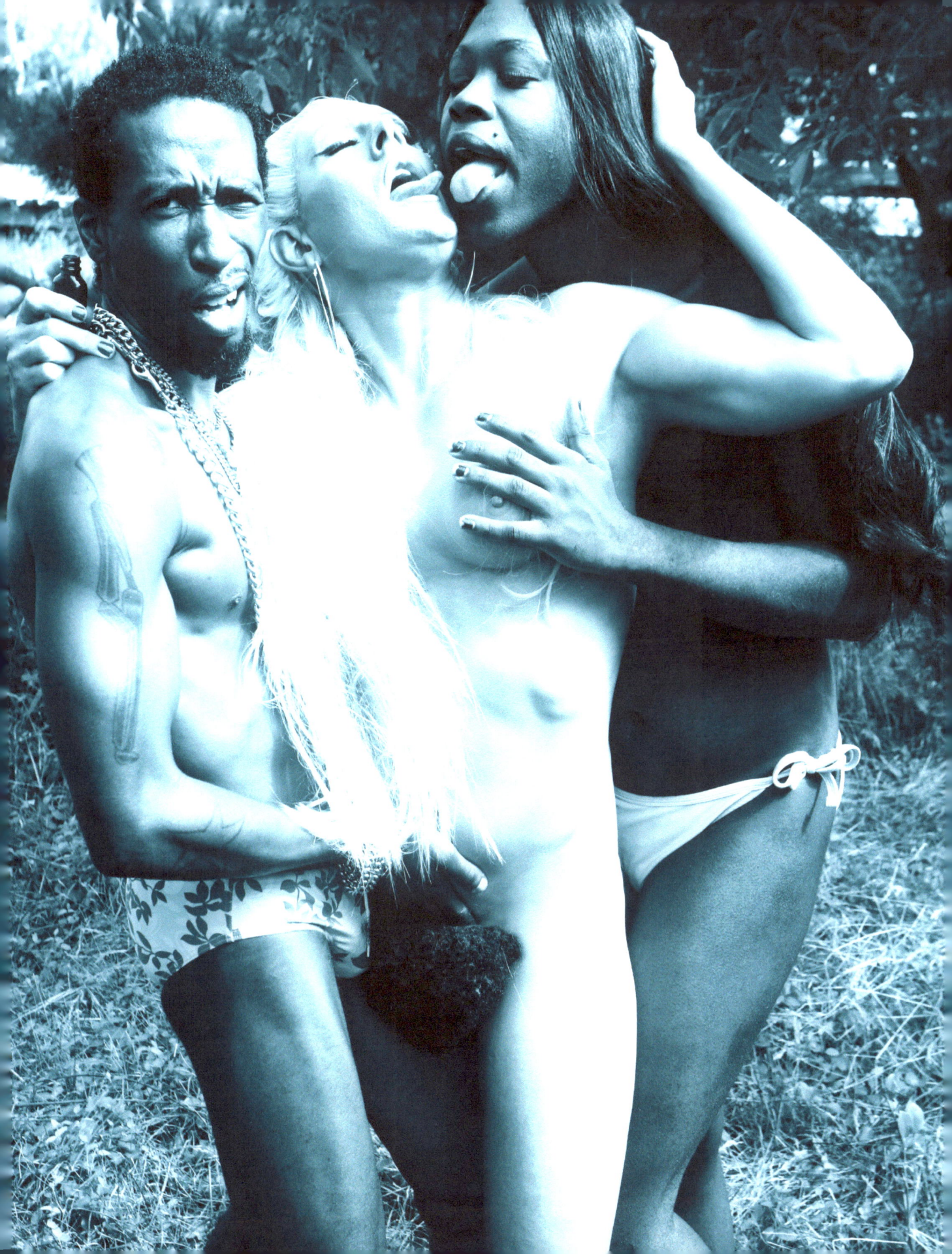

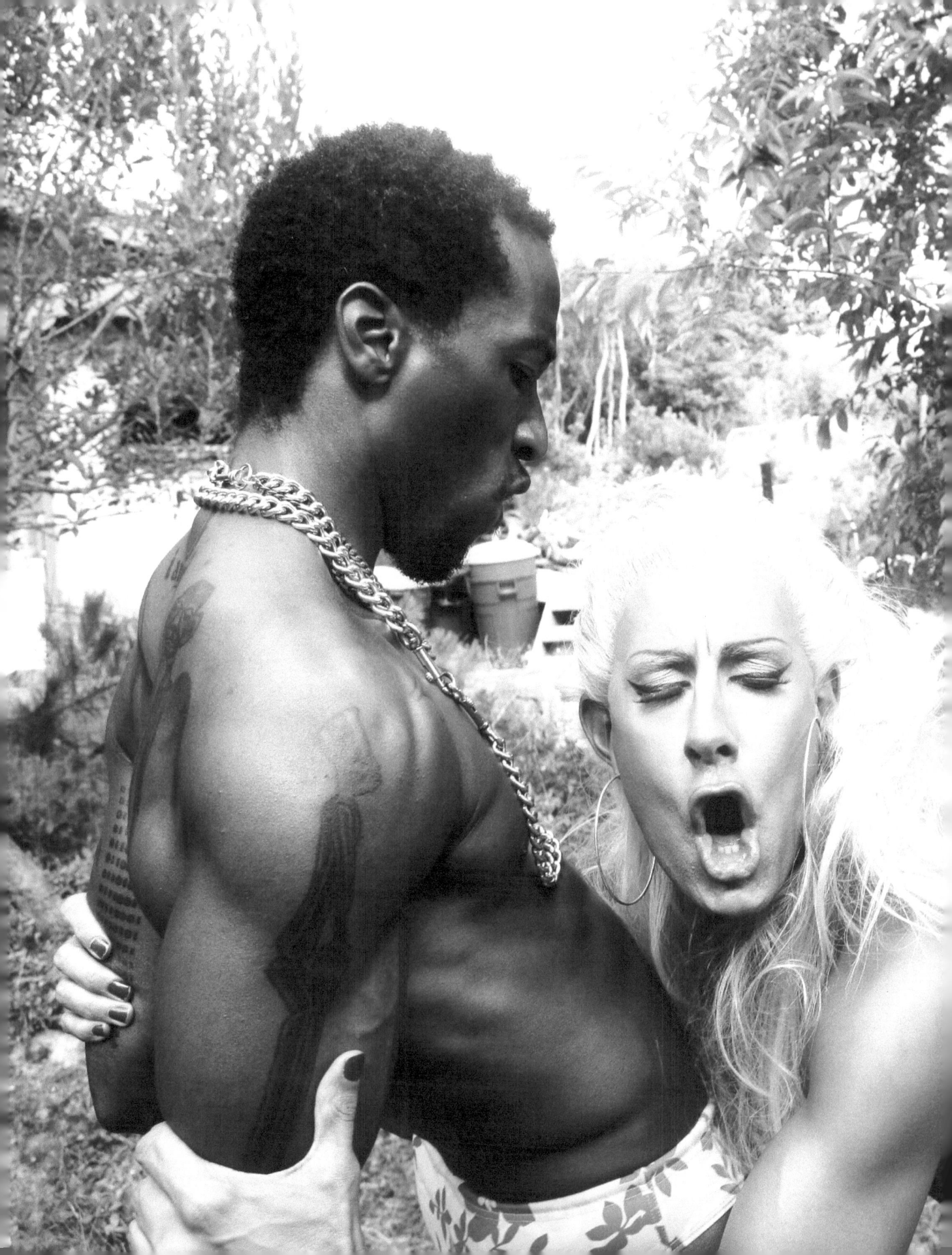

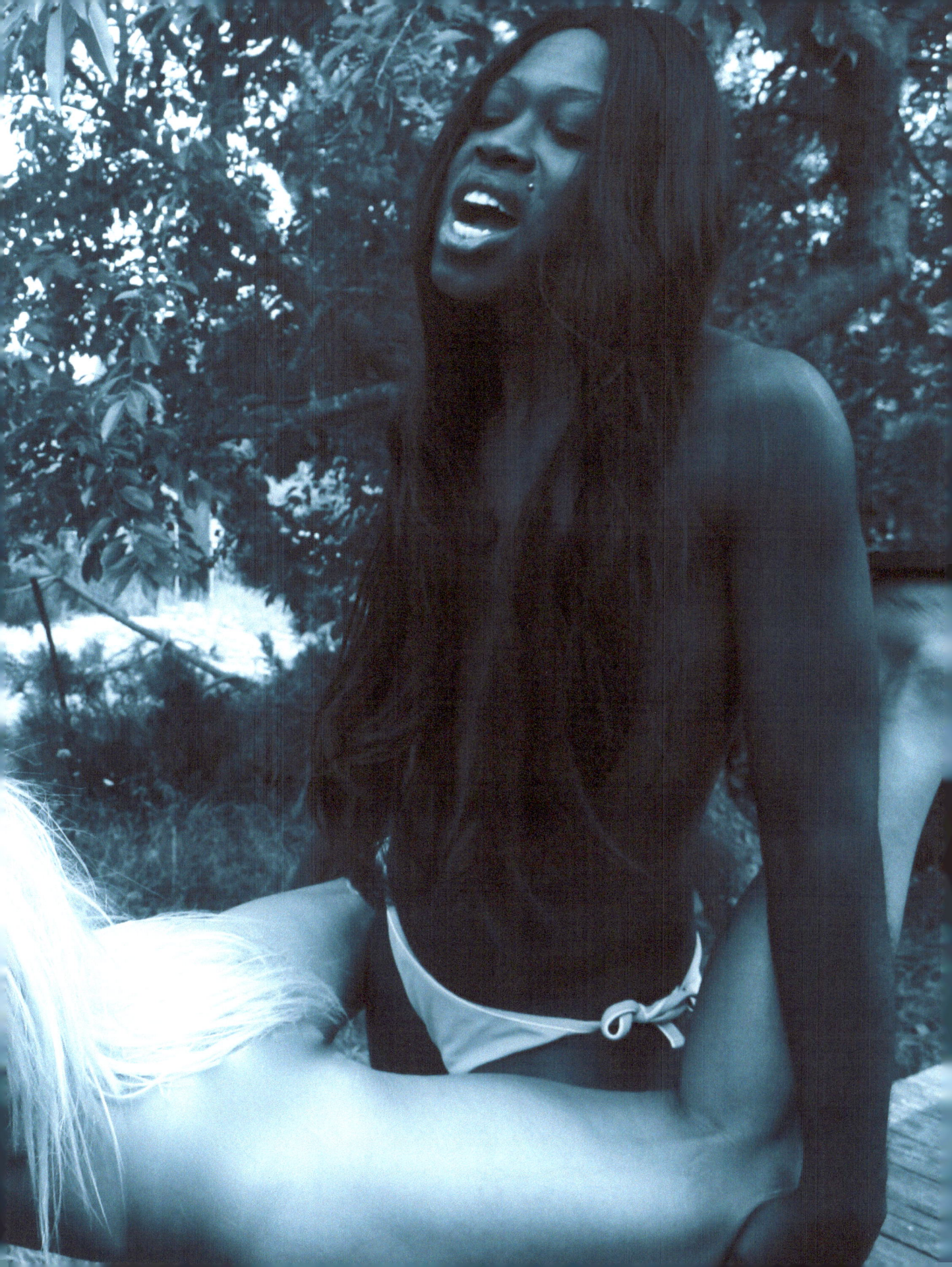

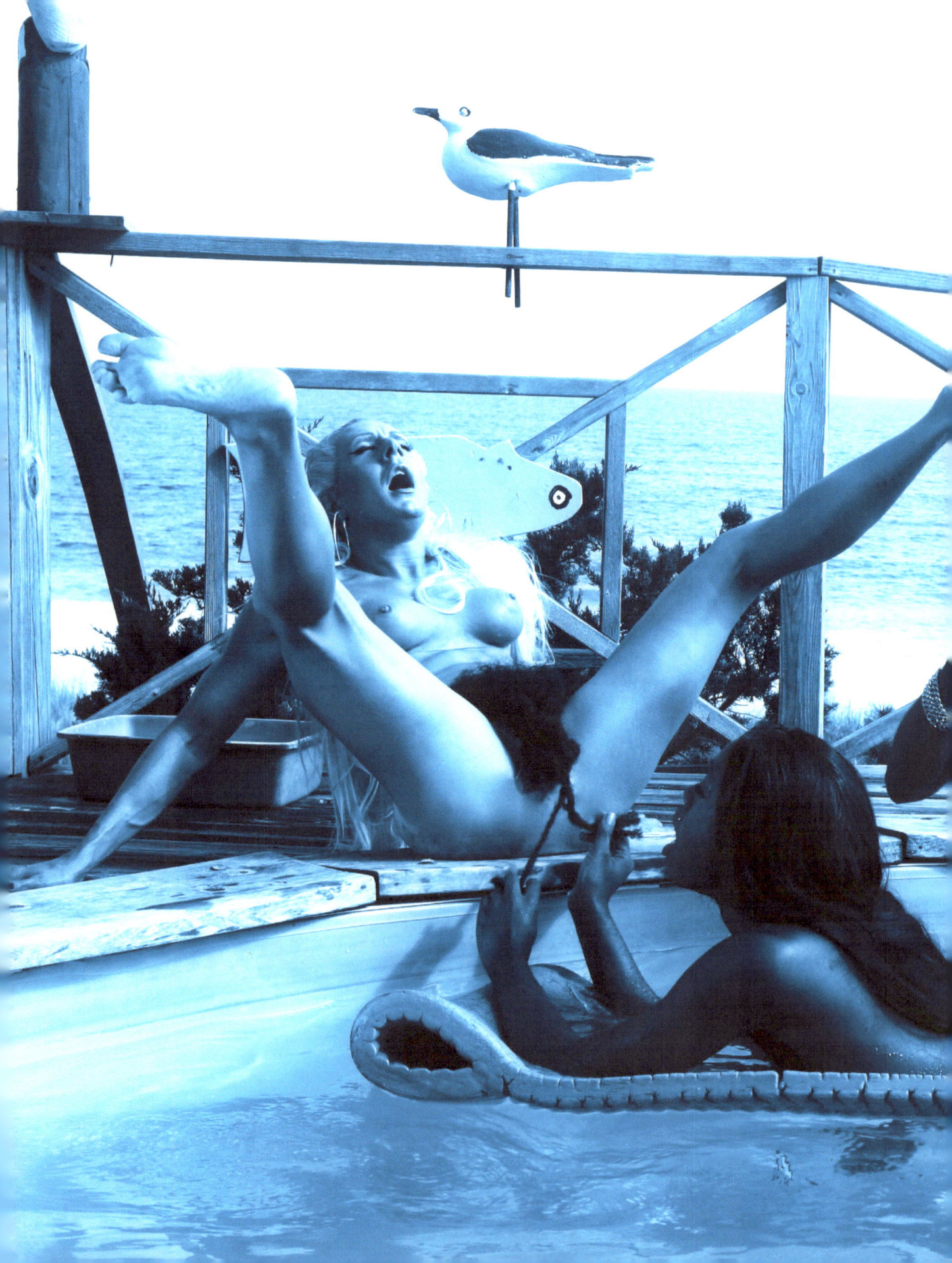

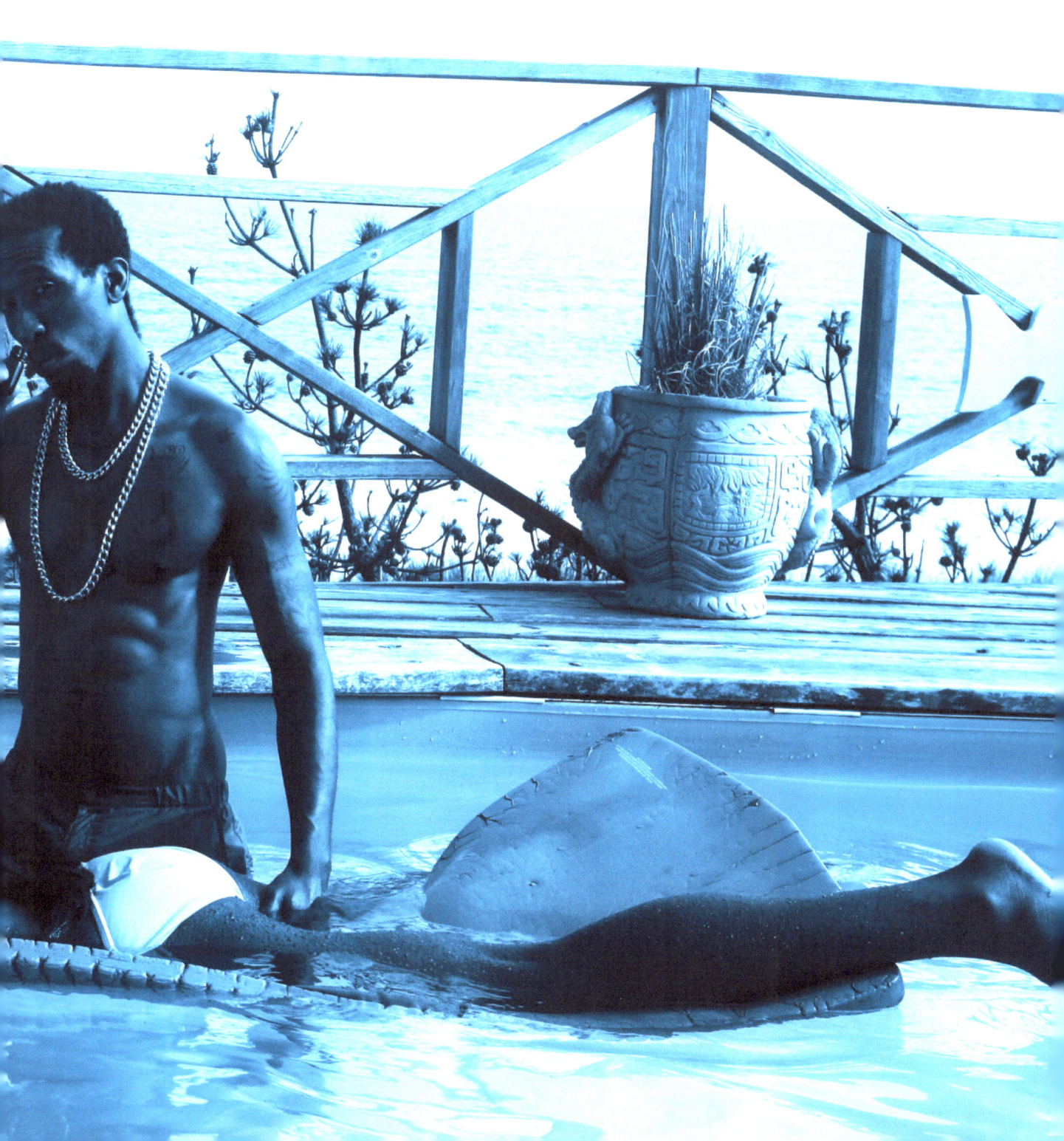

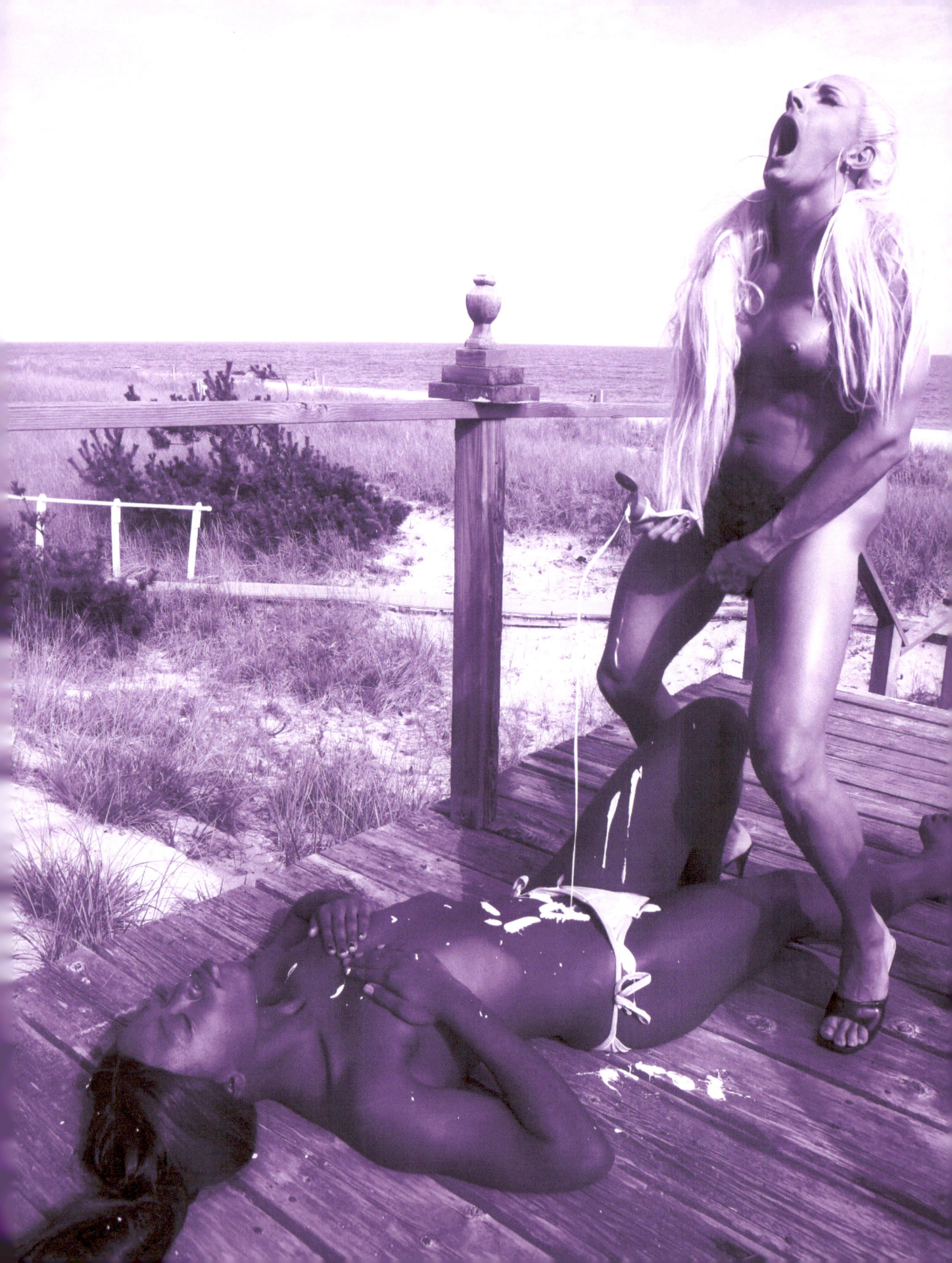

Shoot for the stars!

— Chita

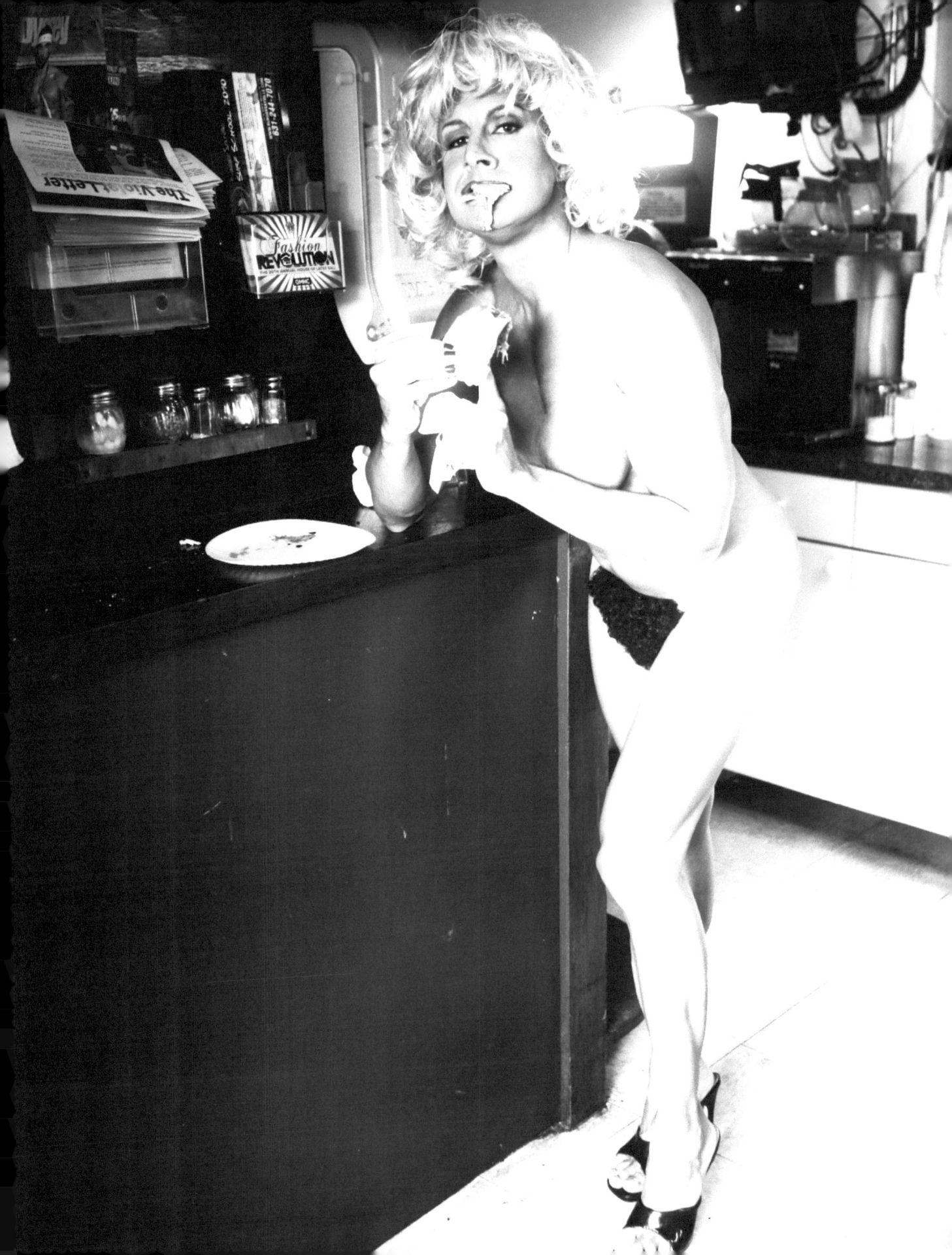

www.ingramcontent.com/pod-product-compliance
Lightning Source LLC
Chambersburg PA
CBHW051201220526
45473CB00003B/859